START YOUR PASSIVE INCOME BUSINESS

Build Your Financial Wealth and Make Money Online Through Retail Arbitrage, E-Commerce, Affiliate Marketing, Dropshipping and Social Media Marketing

Rachel Smith

TABLE OF CONTENTS

INTRODUCTION

Congratulations on purchasing *Start Your Passive Income Business,* and thank you for doing so. It takes considerable time and consideration to find the right book with the answers you are seeking, so please rest assured that your search is over. Know that you have chosen well and will be prepared for the next step: Becoming the boss by building a business that will make money online.

In this book, you will learn about making money online through either active or passive income. In some cases, you may find yourself earning by combining the possibilities of both aspects. In the following chapters, you will be introduced to passive income and how it differs from active, and then learn about several online businesses that you can set up as soon as today. The topics will include whether you need to invest a small sum to get started.

First, you will learn about how to market yourself and your business through social media. This chapter will come with tips, advice on how to get started, and more. Following this chapter will be learning about retail arbitrage. This will include details about how to build a business out of arbitraging and what to look out for when starting.

Next, we discuss dropshipping. This will be a lesson on passive income that has worked for millions of others, so it will work for you if you choose to make this your business. Advice on how to set up the business will be included, as well as tips on the do's and don'ts when dropshipping. The chapter discussing this will fluidly lead to the next chapter due to their relation: Life with E-Commerce. The two subjects are intimately connected. If you choose to run a dropshipping business, then take a close look at the e-commerce section to understand best what you will be doing.

After this, you will learn about a business model that balances active and passive income: Blogging. How to get started, how to maintain it, and other important information will be explained here to ensure your blogging experience is a success. You will also find the chapter that follows, "Connections in Affiliate Marketing," is as relevant to blogging as e-commerce is to dropship. I recommend looking closely at that 8th and final chapter to ensure you are aware of the full potential that both offer to your business.

By the end of this book, you will be equipped with the information needed to get started and left with one final decision that cannot be made for you, but by you: Which business appeals enough for you to get started? Regardless of the direction you take, know that you are ready to take the first steps needed to begin. Good luck with your endeavors.

Because there are plenty of books on this subject on the market, I want to say thanks again for choosing this one! Every effort was made to ensure it is full of as much useful information as possible. Please enjoy!

CHAPTER 1
Making Money Online

A man works hard every day to provide for his wife and two kids. He works from dawn to dusk in hopes of the overtime, giving him that little oomph needed to afford allergy medicine for his youngest. Every month, something comes up that makes overtime a necessary evil. Every month, he feels himself become more and more worn down until he is forced to take a full weekend off so he can rest. When that whole weekend comes, he and his wife sit down to go over the bills and see, once again, they will be short still if he is unable to make up for the 2-day weekend.

He grows tired of working these long hours, but he does not complain because his wife meets this struggle with long hours of her own. She works at a daycare where both of her little ones attend, so her days are filled with the overflowing energy of at least six kids at once. They are both exhausted, but bills are cruel demands from heartless corporations, so they continue working hard to make it all work.

One day, the man hears a new coworker mention they are only working because they wanted an excuse to get out of the house. As he listens to this person talk, he learns about how this person has a business online that brings in more money in the two weeks it takes him to make in a month. It gets him thinking about the Internet and all the websites he and his family visit all the time: Amazon, the New York Times, YouTube. They all make money online.

Could he do it, too? The short answer is yes, but the long answer is a bit more complicated. The extent of his knowledge when using the Internet is Googling questions and watching YouTube for how to fix his car. He is not ready to start his online business yet, so the thought of starting is dismissed for now, but the daydreams of what he could afford and how much time he could dedicate to the kids add a bounce to his step for the rest of the day.

Somewhere else in the country, a young lady is resting at home. She has 2 hours to spare before she needs to be up and out the door to be on time for her part-time, second job, but she is in no hurry. She needs this moment of reprieve to catch her breath because one of the hosts at the restaurant she works at called in, so she doubled as a hostess and a waitress since seven that morning. That job ended a little over half an hour ago. If she allows herself an hour of sleep and has the needed uniform by her bed, then half an hour to get ready should be plenty of time.

As her mind drifts, her thoughts vaguely touch on everything she has done today. Waiting tables for fussy customers is the worst, especially when they refuse to provide a tip. The larger groups are great about leaving tips, but the work that comes with pleasing them overshadows what was earned. Just before sleep claims her, she lets out a soft sigh and remembers just how much she dislikes the job.

By the time she has arrived at the next job, she is reminded how much she dislikes this job, too. It is heavy, physical labor in a warehouse. She must pick and pack orders for 6 hours and gets a single 15-minute break to rest. When she is lucky–though, she often wonders if she can consider it lucky–she is asked to stay for a full 8-hour shift. This is worse than the restaurant, but without it, she would not have any play money for the weekends. The sacrifice must be made so she can have fun.

As rough as the night has been thanks to scanners glitching and printers choosing to be slow, she finds herself not dreading the work as much as usual. During her 15, she was on her phone and happened upon a site that offered jobs that would let her work from home, and even better, it advertised that she could work on her own time. She could be the boss of her days and still earn everything needed for bills and fun.

A tantalizing idea, but like the man who works from dawn to dusk, she is unfamiliar with the concept. It sounded too good to be true, and she knew that the Internet was full of dangers, too. For all she knew, this was a scheme to get her to pay for nonexistent opportunities that would waste her time and money. Still, she had to wonder, so when she returned to work, she could not resist talking about it.

"What an impossible thing," she tells her friend as they race together to pick an exceptionally large order; "Making enough money online not to need jobs like this." She was grateful to be working with her friend on this order. The timing was great, and she was sure her friend would not tease her about feeling even a little hopeful.

"Anything is possible," her friend replies after they finish rearranging the pallet, so everything fits on it. There was a light in her friend's eyes that revealed genuine interest in the idea. "Honestly, I would love to try it. Want to look into it together, Friday night?" They often spend the weekends together, so the offer was no surprise.

"You know," she eventually replies as they begin wrapping the pallet with shrink wrap. "Why not? It could be fun. Not everything online could be a scam."

Not Everything is a Scam

As you well know, that off-handed remark is true: Not everything is a scam online. If we continue to follow these stories, then we would watch as both parties learn more about the possibilities to make money online, and we would eventually read about their successes. The stories would have promoted patience, diligence, and self-discipline. If the stories from earlier expanded upon, you would have joined them in the ups and downs of learning how to make the Internet work for them.

For example, the man who started daydreaming at work; every night he was home, he did his research little by little until, finally, he found an idea that could work for him. With the support of his wife, he got started, and he worked to build it up in any free time he could find. The married couple now runs a blog that promotes and shares their adventures as parents, a family, and summer-travel enthusiasts.

At the same time, the young lady who talked about how impossible making money online seemed to her did join her coworker in building a business online. When they got together that night to hang out, her friend came with research done and exciting stories about the possibilities to share. They had their fair share of up-and-downs, and a few times they were lost about what steps they were missing, but they eventually found success. In the end, that young lady and her coworker went on to build a fashionable e-commerce website. To this day, they still run it together, and they found a second business module, dropshipping, that almost entirely runs itself.

These successes are within your grasp just as much as it was in theirs: You need only dig a little deeper and see what you need to get started. There are many ways to make money online, such as writing books or making videos for all to enjoy. If you take a minute to check Google, Bing, or what-have-you, then you would see that many online opportunities are also offered by well-known companies. For example, companies are always searching for social media marketers or capable of writers to help pitch their products and services. You need only look to see it for what it is: An opportunity for you to grasp.

Know What You Want

The main trick to know before you get started is deciding what you can or want to do to make money online. Do you want to run a business of your own, or are you fine working for an established company? If you are interested in working for established companies but do not have experience with what they are looking for, you can pitch yourself as a freelance worker.

This allows you to set preferred rates. However, this requires you to contact companies yourself and make cold pitches to show that you have a topic relevant to what they and their customers are interested in. This is a difficult and advanced path to take due to the level of preparation needed, the devastating lack of replies from contacted clients, and the unending struggle to get clients to pay you for your work. Because of how advanced and how much work is required to become a professional freelancer, it is recommended you start with business models that will be discussed here.

It may seem impossible where you are now, but it does not have to stay this way. In the very word, "impossible" is the phrase, "I'm possible." If you believe in the impossible, then you can believe in yourself, too. That said, you must not rush into this endeavor. Starting a business, both online and in-person, requires time, research about what your business will specialize in, and an understanding of the legalities and tax expectations of having your own business.

Rushing the Income

This requires patience, perseverance, and self-discipline. If you "rush the income," as certain professionals have put it, then you will find yourself burnt out from experience long before you have completed the necessary preparations to succeed. The burn out can be strong when you run headfirst into this, so remember to take it slow. The impatience or excessive eagerness to succeed are recipes leading to failure and must be held in check during the entire process. If it gets the better of you for even a moment, you may find yourself questioning why it is taking so long to get anywhere with your business.

Another common issue is losing interest in the early stages. When you are not accustomed to working online, you may find yourself lapsing into the common state of wanting instant gratification. It is something we all experience due to how easy technology has made life. When we are hungry but do not wish to cook, for example, food is easily produced by putting an order to a restaurant via a phone app, a website, or a phone call.

Starting your business will not be as easy as ordering a pizza or burger with fries. It will require the discipline you have developed for your day (or night if you work graveyard) job. In some cases, it may require your best customer service voice. The discipline you have gained during your time in the workforce, will be tested by choice to start an online business—your discipline, as well as your perseverance.

Work can be devastating some days and then motivating on others. Regardless of how it starts and how much you may think about quitting because you deserve better, you always choose to keep going because it is just a few hours longer. When you have your online business set up, it may be slow in the beginning. This will be because you are a new business, so you lack the traffic needed to spread the word of your presence. There are several ways to change this, but you will have to be persistent to make any of them work. An example of how to attract attention to your business will be marketing yourself via social media—assuming; you do not choose to make social media marketing your online career.

Marketing yourself via social media is a popular tactic used by every business. The trick, however, is knowing how to sell your products or services to ensure customers develop and stay interested in your line of business. In later chapters, turning social media marketing into a career will be explained in greater detail. That will provide the opportunity to deepen your understanding of how marketing works, what practices have proven to work best, and whether choosing to do social media marketing is the career path for you or if you should continue with building your brand.

Assuming you continue to create your own business, you must consider the available options. Once again, not all online opportunities are scams, though there are plenty of examples that scream "scam!" One such online technique is a popular idea that has been around for years: The "pyramid scheme." Know that this business model is illegal and that it involves new investors to pay upfront to join. If you find yourself encouraged to pay some fee to join a business, then make an informed decision by researching what this company does and if anyone else has experience with them.

If you are still uncertain about what business you want to run, then consider the following: retail arbitrage, dropshipping, running an e-commerce business, or stepping into the blogging world. Each choice provides advantages and disadvantages to consider, so once again, you are encouraged to make informed decisions before deciding on a path.

Examples of Online Ventures

For example, retail arbitrage ensures that you have goods that are always in demand. A drawback to this business includes the requirement to physically go out to obtain the demanded goods so you can sell them online. If you choose to dropship, however, then you would not need any physical goods stored to sell. Instead, you will have to consistently research ongoing trends to make sure your dropshipping store stays relevant.

One of the best ways to make money online is by having a business that provides a passive income. The only downfall to passive income is that it still counts as taxable income like the other business options, so remember to save money on the side to afford the taxes that come with earning money. Regardless of what business you choose to run, be sure you save some of your earnings to file the required taxes.

Because the business will be yours, you will be responsible for both the employer and employee payroll taxes. You will be considered self-employed, meaning you will pay the full 15.3% taxes on all net earnings. According to the IRS, that is divided between social security, which adds up to 12.4%, and Medicare, which is the remaining 2.9%. After a certain amount earned, the taxed amount for Medicare will increase by a rate of 0.9%. It is recommended to rely on a tax expert to handle this paperwork. The recommended businesses in this book are all beginner-friendly, so do not feel intimidated about getting started. The pros and cons of each business will not be overwhelming compared to more advanced businesses, such as being a freelance worker. When getting started, it is also easier to set up these businesses, and it does not generally require much monetary investment to start, if any money at all.

Later chapters will also go into greater detail about each choice. By the end of this book, you should feel like an expert on the mentioned business models and ready to try one for yourself. That said, if you feel none quite fit what you believe will help you make money online, then know that these are not the all-encompassing choices available. As previously mentioned, these are beginner-friendly choices. The reason these are considered friendly to beginners is that they do not require you to be particularly skilled or savvy to make any of them work for you.

If you are looking to utilize skills that you have, such as painting, sewing, or technical writing, then know that there are businesses where you can put these skills to use. Such businesses may prove more advanced than what is offered here, but what you learn here can and will apply to your more advanced interests. If you plan to sell your work, for example, you will still be expected to either make or join a website where you can sell the paintings, handiwork, etc.

Keep Your Day Job

To help you get started, make sure you consider your interests and whether they can be used to make money online. If you find nothing you are interested in will work at first, then it is okay to rely on the beginner-friendly business models suggested in this book. That said, if you do not feel strongly about any of the choices offered here, then remember that there are other options available as well. These are just the easiest ways to get started online.

Regardless of what business you choose to set up online, be sure not to quit your day job while you start up your online business. The money you make online will not be enough to replace your day job at first, so you must not quit your regular job in hopes of this taking over. In the beginning, making money online will start as a side hustle, something that you do in your free time.

Your day job will continue to be the main source of your income for some time. So, while it is fine to contemplate ways to improve your online business while you are working your regular job, make sure it does not get in the way of your production levels and undermine your expected work ethic. Allowing your work ethic to slip can and will cause strife at the workplace for you because your boss and your coworkers will start noticing your production levels slipping.

Your bosses will always be quick to notice when someone is not working as hard as usual and will not waste time questioning where your focus has gone. If you do not have a valid excuse for why you are slipping up or slowing down at work, your position in the company may be threatened. Do not give them a reason to doubt your work ethic because you are too busy daydreaming about the possibilities with your online business.

It is best to dedicate any time after work or on your days off to your online business. Though you may feel the business is slow to get started and make money, it will ensure your day job is safe. To ensure you do not burn out on the idea of running your business online, do not dedicate more time to it than you would dedicate to a hobby until the business begins to pick up in earnest.

During the weekdays, you must not dedicate more than 3 or 4 evenings to the online business. If you set up a schedule to help you stay on track about when you can work on the business, as well as what aspect of the business you will focus on during those times. Splitting up the workload with a schedule like this will guarantee success.

Also, while you will have more time on your weekends to work on the online business, it is not recommended to fill your weekend with it. Dedicating your weekends to it can leave you feeling overall burnt out because you will not have any time to rest, so your ability and desire to continue with this venture will rapidly deplete. It will feel like you no longer have days off and can take time away from your family or friends, which is bad for your mental health and may diminish your interest due to feeling isolated.

Conflict of Interest

A word of caution for when balancing your day job and your online business: If they are in similar fields, you may want to check to see whether running your business on the side will be considered a conflict of interest with your day job. Conflict of interest is a technical term used in business to explain how an individual may be in a situation where continuing to pursue the side business makes the individual a direct competitor with his or her employer.

This situation often leads to the employee being dismissed from the job to protect the company's business practices and trade secrets. Before you take the plunge to start your business, make sure you speak with your Human Resource department to know whether you signed any contracts stating you cannot work for a competing company. An example would be having you sign an agreement upon hire or orientation.

This form typically states you will not be employed by/become a competing company within X amount of days, with X being a specific time frame chosen by the company. If your employer determines that your interests are no longer aligned with the company's, then you run a high chance of being let go. The usual reason the company uses to warrant this action is claiming that your loyalties are in question, and continuing to employ you will endanger the company's competitive edge. An example of finding yourself becoming a form of competition to your employer would see the raw goods your employer orders and, because you know the quality is good, choosing to buy them as well to improve your products. This is taking advantage of what your job has to offer and using their trade secrets to give your own business an advantage in the market.

Overall, it is a hassle to find yourself in a situation that can put you in a precarious position of conflicting interests. It is best to either completely avoid becoming competition against your employer or to do your due diligence by researching and speaking with professionals on what is and is not acceptable.

CHAPTER 2
Introducing Passive Income

Making money online is a popular concept, and though there are millions of ways to get started, the idea of how to make money without putting in the same hours at work is always skimmed over. No one has an extra 8+ hours in the workweek to dedicate to this venture, and for those people who do have that extra time on their hands, it is reasonable to assume they would not be thrilled to do it anyway.

Because of this, among the popular ideas thrown around online is making passive money online. A quick Google about how to make money online will always bring up links that talk about passive income ideas that can make you $1,000 every month and more. The thought of making $1,000 every month without having to work a second or third job doing it is tempting.

For many individuals, it is a difficult concept to accept. This is because, as mentioned in the previous chapter, there are scams all over the Internet that hope to get money from you with promises that it will pay off for you. Those scams certainly exist, but the ability to make passive income online is real and legitimate. What, then, is passive income, and what is so special?

Understanding Passive Income

Passive income is a relatively loose term to encompass how diverse your options are for earning money that is not an active income. In short, passive income is money earned and maintained while requiring little to no activity from you. The business essentially runs and builds itself, providing you the option to focus your efforts and time in other ventures, such as your day job or your family life.

Money earned passively like this is technically taxable because it is still a source of income, though it is treated differently by financial advisors and the Internal Revenue Service (IRS). Taxes for passive income is relatively lower than income earned through jobs and may be more complicated than the standard deduction filing. It is often recommended you have a professional file your taxes when you have passive income involved.

The reason this is advised is that the IRS has a specific definition for what constitutes passive income, so the loose term provided earlier may include other income types that also have established definitions from the IRS. One such income that is often included in the passive spectrum is portfolio income. Money earned in a portfolio income includes investments, interest, or royalties.

A common understanding of passive income involves investing your money in ventures that guarantee cash-flow. By the IRS's understanding, this income requires you to have little to no participation in earning money. So, while it is true that dividends and peer-to-peer lending (P2P) ventures are passive income because you are not required to put great effort into either, the IRS will most likely disagree.

Passive income has steadily gained popularity over the years due to the cost of living growing faster than wages. The money made from passive income is a welcomed boost to active income that is overburdened by the growing inflation. After you have grown your passive income enough to overshadow your active income, you can consider whether you want to continue with your active income or if you want to work from home through your passive income.

Active and Passive Income

Where passive income requires next to no involvement, active income requires some form of involvement that is legally acknowledged as material participation. Material participation is a fancy term explaining that states you have actively earned income through a business by providing either services or products to its customers. In this way, your active income will always include salaries, tips, wages, and other incomes that are earned from working with that company.

Your day job is your active income. If you have a gig job like driving for Uber or DoorDash, then your gig job is also an active income. Anything that requires you to put in the effort to earn an income counts as an active income; investing in stocks, ETFs, or bonds can be considered active or passive. The determining factor is your method of investing.

When actively investing, you must put in the extra work to research what investments are best to buy into, then turning around to wholesale your investments. Wholesaling is a popular strategy often found in real estate and is better known as "flipping." When you wholesale, you are essentially paid for finding an impressive investment and selling the investment for profit to other interested investors.

Taking this route in investing makes the process a job. This is because you are spending a great amount of time hunting for deals and then hunting for investors who would pay a premium for the investments you have available. Many people seem to think this does not count as a job because it is investing, but the time spent to make it work the facts.

That said, it is possible to turn active investments into passive ones. If you are investing and wholesaling, you could put your profit into passive investments. Passive investments generate income without the need for your input and effort, making them ideal for busy individuals who have full-time jobs. With enough money invested in your passive investments, you can quit your wholesaling job and let the passive revenue keep you afloat from then on.

Pros and Cons of Active VS Passive

One of the greatest advantages of active income over passive is the stability of it. You can always count on your next paycheck and predict what you will get because you know the hours and wages provided by your company. If you run a gig job, you set your hours and can actively choose to earn the income needed to pay bills. That predictability is stable and allows you to plan finances accordingly. You guarantee your bills will be paid and know when you will have extra money to put elsewhere every time.

The same cannot be said about passive income. Passive income can be volatile compared to active. This depends on the market that you invested in, like the real estate or stock market. If the market is standing strong and growing, then your investments are safe. But if doubt is thrown into the market due to political movements, the Federal Reserve making changes to interest rates or other hiccups in the economy, your investments can and will suffer.

When you rely on a specific market, you may find yourself going long periods with low cash-flow. This is a disadvantage that both types of income suffer from. For active income, your specific market is your place of employment. If you wanted to cushion this source of income, you could either find a passive income or seek another job. This struggle of multiplying sources of income does not affect passive income, however.

To ensure your passive income stays strong, you must diversify your investments. This way, you are not relying on a specific market to keep you afloat. Diversifying your investments can also stagger when your money flows into your accounts. This way, when one source is negatively impacted by reasons outside of your control, you will still have the other investments to rely on. Diversifying is also made easier with passive income because your options are not limited by time constraints and qualifications.

The greatest advantage of passive income compared to active is the unlimited potential for earnings. Because you can easily diversify your passive income, you can feasibly create enough sources of cash-flow to overshadow your active income. Passive income can grow exponentially without you having to lift a finger, but active income does not have that luxury.

Active income has several limits, like time in the day. No matter how hard and fast you work, there will always be only 24 hours in the day, and you cannot possibly work all 24 hours. You are also limited by your wages. Even a gig worker can provide so many services or produce so much content in a day before having to rest. Passive income never rests.

Though passive income never rests, it is a slow riser. It requires time to make enough passive revenue to live on. Depending on how you earn the passive income, you may find yourself making pennies to a handful of dollars in the first few months, perhaps even years. You must also be careful about your plan of action. If your passive income comes from investing, you must be prepared to sit and wait for your money to grow on its own.

This is the worst part about relying on passive income: The reality that your income is truly passive. It is usual for people to grow bored from earning passive income, especially after years of having to work hard for every cent received. This passivity is why everyone continues to work available day jobs. Even working a minimum wage, a part-time job is better than sitting at home doing nothing.

That said, the ability to work any job you feel like working is freeing thanks to passive income. You will always rest easy knowing you do not need this job because your passive income is enough to live on. The active income you earn is your excuse to go out and socialize, making it more enjoyable to work.

Importance of Mindset

How you tackle the task of building up your passive income and whether you will successfully achieve your goal to make money online depending on your mindset. With a positive and unwavering mindset, you are more likely to succeed. Your mindset is what determines your spending, earning, and saving habits.

For example, if you live "paycheck to paycheck," then you may have a frugal mindset because every cent and dollar determines whether you meet a bill. This mindset can make you fearful of overspending, which leaves you unable to invest in opportunities that can rescue you from your situation, or frivolous because you want the luxury of living your best life despite not having the funds to maintain the appearance.

Another common mindset that will get in the way of success is a procrastinating one. Procrastination is a disadvantageous mindset that is arguably worse than being frugal or frivolous with your money. Individuals who tend to procrastinate often struggle or fail to meet their goals and tasks. These struggles and failures will worsen the mindset and lead the individual to procrastinate even further, ending in a cycle of failures and avoidance of work because of the fear of failing.

In order to overcome a procrastination mindset, it is important to know the root cause of why you choose to procrastinate. Are you frightened by failure? Perhaps the idea of success is intimidating because you do not know what to do from there? A few common root causes include low self-esteem, negative thinking, and the struggle with perfectionism.

When you are aware of what is preventing you from getting on-task, you must confront yourself and lay out your goals. You know what you want and know you can get it with time and effort. If your low self-esteem belittles your efforts, then consider appeasing it by breaking larger projects into smaller, more manageable ones. When your low self-esteem flares, you can convince yourself to complete one small project and call it good.

If your negative thinking is the problem, then reward yourself with a break so you can step away from the project. When you allow yourself distance from it to focus on your needs, you allow yourself to see the project with fresh eyes that will see how far you have come and how well you have done. Negative thinking is a hassle we all suffer from, but it can be soothed by taking time to take care of yourself.

Finally, if perfectionism is the issue, then create a list of what needs to be done and when. Force yourself to stick to those deadlines and accept that what you have accomplished is acceptable for the timeframe you were allowed. Your perfectionism can handle the deadlines, and you may surprise yourself with how well everything works out after you take a step back to look over your progress.

With the right mindset, you can achieve your financial goals and succeed at making money online. You will not be afraid to spend money on investments because you will succeed in your venture. You will not frivolously spend it because you have a goal in mind and a plan to achieve it.

Getting into the right mindset can be tricky when you are not primed to be ambitious about finances. The correct mindset you need is abundant. This means you are looking for an abundance of opportunities and are confident about what the future holds. This mindset lacks the fears and carelessness of the previous mindsets and is instead focused on the prize.

Improving Your Mindset

Improving your mindset to make money online, both actively and passively, boils down to your determination and how well you can make a change stick. This will require discipline and patience you might demonstrate only at work because you are expected to behave in certain ways while on the job. Use the skills you have developed from working to improve your mindset and prepare yourself for making money online.

An important change to your mindset to ensure success is adjusting the importance of proving yourself to everyone. People who spend frivolously have it conditioned in their heads that the display of having money to spend makes them attractive and successful. These people live in illusions, often because they are disappointed in their situations, and are likely running away from their problems.

Do not be like these people. Having money may be a symbol of power and envy, but this desire to use it to impress others should not be your goal. By striving to be successful in the eyes of your peers, you privately admit that you are not successful and, therefore, financially powerless. That need to compensate for your powerlessness is the wrong mindset to bear. It also leads you to constantly comparing yourself to your peers, which makes for a devastating and weak mindset for making money in general.

15

Looking around at work, friends, social media, and celebrities, it can be easy to become envious of others' positions. When you compare yourself to the people around you and the successes they have achieved, you put yourself at an unfair disadvantage.

For one, you are comparing your entire self–successes and failures combined–to the successes that these people choose to show. You do not know how hard they worked or how long it took for them to reach that position. You also do not know what failures they overcame to reach that point. Instead of comparing your entire self, compare your successes instead.

Worst of all, by taking the time to make these comparisons, you are losing time for your financial goals. How can you make money online if you are entertaining jealous thoughts about your friend and his new truck? Your financial aspirations will not achieve themselves–especially if you are just starting to build your business or passive income.

You must dismiss what is happening in your peers' lives to focus on yourself. They will always be nearby, succeeding, and failing, so there is no need to waste a second of your time on them. How well your product or service is received online is more important at this moment. For the next step, your next big goal takes priority.

Focus on what needs to be done. With set goals in mind, you can direct your energy and finances to achieve these goals. It is practical to assign your money to specific tasks that will help you move from step-to-step. Having direction for your finances makes staying focused easier and prevents you from falling into frivolous or fearful habits.

Your focus will also prevent you from spending based on emotions. When something exciting takes place, the first thought is often celebrating the event. Celebrations typically cost money, which takes away from your goals. It is fine to occasionally spend on celebrations because you are in high spirits and can train this positive energy to further empower your goals by making money online.

But it is not okay to spend when you are devastated. Negative spending happens more than positive spending, and this poor mindset makes it easy to overspend by mistake. Life has its ups, downs, and its curveballs, so the desire to ease your hurt or need to feel in control again can tempt you to spend unnecessarily.

You must resist this urge. Mistakes happen in life, and while we cannot take them back, we can use them as examples of what to do better. Instead of wallowing about your loss of control, forgive yourself for making a mistake. By practicing self-forgiveness, you make it easier to look at the situation without negative bias. Forgiveness allows you to see what went wrong, understand how, and accept what needs to be done. You do not trap yourself in the past when you can forgive mistakes, thus allowing you to move forward without weight on your shoulders.

Options to Start Passively Earning

With your mindset focused, the second-largest hurdle is determining what you need to get started. In certain cases, you will need to spend money to make money. This is not to say you should believe those scams that have you spending large amounts just for empty promises. No, the money you spend should go to investments that will get either your online business or your passive income started.

An example of money spent correctly is investing in real estate. There are online platforms that will allow you to invest in commercial and residential properties from the comforts of your home. For investing in real estate, a crowd favorite is RealtyMogul: A crowdfunding platform that has been around long enough to be considered a high quality, low-risk investment marketplace for real estate.

With the proper research, you may find RealtyMogul is known for vetting their sponsors and ensuring every part of every made deal is done with value in mind. This particular platform offers a diversified array of real estate to invest in, and it offers portfolio and asset management, so you will always know the value of your investments 24/7.

To get started on a site like RealtyMogul, however, you will need money for investing. The minimum to start at RealtyMogul is $5,000, and though that amount may seem daunting, the platform has proven its legitimacy with time and overall success. Similar sites may ask for more to start, so choosing to get into real estate should be a more advanced step in your online money-making venture.

That said, there are more financially friendly means of starting a business or passive income venture online. If you are unwilling or unable to spend money to get an online venture started, then consider ideas that utilize what you have on hand, such as the camera on your phone. There are platforms such as Getty Images or Shutterstock.

If you like to take pictures when you go on vacation or just see something that is pretty at the time, then selling stock photos is a viable start to making money online. With how easy it is to take a picture on your phone, creating a passive income from selling stock photos on sites like the above mentioned is easy and costs nothing. The only know-how you need is how to upload your pictures to the websites.

Once your pictures are out there, you are done. Customers who use the website–or sites if you choose to post on multiple platforms–will do the work for you. They know what photos they want, and if yours happens to be the one, then you will be paid each time a customer chooses to use it. Depending on the site you upload your photos on, you can earn anywhere from 15% to 45% royalties on each download. With enough photos uploaded on enough sites, those royalties can add up swiftly.

Other popular means to earn passively online include the dropshipping business, which is e-commerce made self-efficient, and affiliate marketing. These options require minimal effort to get started and a similar effort to maintain. Between the two, affiliate marketing will require more effort because it requires you to promote products and services to earn a profit.

If you do not have a business or website to advertise on, promoting your sponsor can be difficult. Choosing to be an affiliate marketer can also require monthly costs to maintain. At a minimum, the average monthly cost can add up to roughly $500. For dropshipping, you do have the option to start for free. If you do not know what you are doing or how to get started, then involving a third-party to help set up your dropshipping business would be better. Utilizing a third-party will require money upfront. It can cost anywhere from $14 to $500 a month, so weigh your options carefully.

There are numerous ways to passively make money online, but again, a downfall to relying on passive income is the lack of personal activity involved. It is difficult to feel like you have achieved anything when you find yourself doing nothing to earn it. Therefore, it is increasingly common for people to make money online to choose more active businesses. These businesses include marketing products or services on social media, going out to practice retail arbitrage, building e-commerce, or blogging.

CHAPTER 3
Social Media Marketing And You

Although social media marketing was mentioned as an active means to make money online, it can be altered to be passive, too. This is dependent on preference and how much you are willing to spend to make it work one way versus the other. If debating whether you want to start your own business, social media marketing will be one of the key components to drawing in customers.

On the same note, you can build a business out of social media marketing and find clients in need of your expertise. The social media marketing venture is also flexible enough to choose the third option if the first two are not appealing. You could apply as a social media marketer for existing companies.

Before you decide which path you want to take, first understand what social media marketing is, the basics, and how it is relevant to your interests. Put simply; social media marketing is advertising a company's or your business' products and services by using social media websites and networks. These websites can include Facebook, Instagram, and more. The networks include LinkedIn for professionals and Twitter for general use.

Social media marketing is also a term used interchangeably with digital marketing and e-marketing. If you choose to work for a company or advertise your social media marketing business, expect to see these three terms used in the job and business descriptions. Digital marketers are expected to improve companies' relations with their customer bases, reach new customers, and promote the companies' cultures and missions.

It is the marketer's job to engage with the public in a way that makes the company more respectable and improve brand loyalty. In order to do this, marketers are expected to understand how to read and utilize data analytics tools that determine the successes and weaknesses of their marketing. Depending on how well they do, the marketers will be expected to engage the masses in new and clever ways every day.

The companies that employ these experts regularly expect a broad range of strategies, tactics, and innovative content that will positively engage the customers. Due to their importance in promoting the company, social media marketers are given a broad range of information to help them target the specific audiences who would be most interested in the company's products and services. This information includes customers' personal information that is collected online, as well as their demographic and geographic information.

Social Media Marketing Today

If the idea of starting an e-marketing business proves intimidating, but you still find interest in becoming a digital marketer, then applying for an established company is a solid start to making money online. All companies have used experts at marketing and using social media, so finding a job should be effortless. Getting the job, however, is another story because you will need proof that you will succeed. Examples of companies that use social media marketing include, but are not limited to, Airbnb, Amazon, and Netflix.

Airbnb's marketers proved their worth when they won the masses over by supporting the masses during a global pandemic in a way only they could: Providing lodgings for first responders when the hospitality industry was in a flummox. Amazon's marketers continue to win over the customers with their entertaining and clever use of social media. Social media marketers for Amazon have found a clever balance between advertising their products while also subtly promoting others, which easily wins people over by making them feel special for getting a response *and* a boost in views.

Finally, Netflix's marketers wowed its customers and improved the loyalty rating of subscribers with a brilliant strategy. During the global pandemic, Netflix sought to unite people despite the distances and help everyone maintain positive mental health. These social media marketers shared information and helped Netflix launch a series that allowed the public to connect with mental health experts to get the answers and help needed to stay strong during those trying times.

As you can see, social media marketers have online charisma that can be irresistible. If you believe yourself to be equally charismatic because you often find yourself leading the team or being chosen to help represent a sponsor or your company, then making money online as a social media marketer may be right for you.

Becoming a Social Media Marketer

If you have determined that digital marketing is for you, then the next step is to learn what you need to become an expert social media marketer. For a resume, there are several essential skills, traits, and experiences you should add to show that you are qualified for the position. To start, you must prove that you have excellent writing skills.

Your ability to write influences whether you have the skills to communicate with the masses effectively. This is a core skill that makes or breaks the digital marketer. The ability to engage in compelling conversations while using the brand's preferred voice–fun and witty like Amazon's or encouraging and welcoming like Netflix's–is key to a social media marketer's success.

You must know how to grab a customer's attention with your writing and inspire the desired emotions in them within the few seconds a viewer spends on ads. This plays into the next skill that is crucial for e-marketing experts: Communication. At the core of social media platforms and networks is the need or desire to communicate with others. As an expert on marketing on social media, you are required to have the skills to effectively communicate what the company has to offer.

The communication skills you present must be flexible because you will oversee bringing the company's voice to several platforms, media, and audiences. The tone you carry on Twitter will be more relaxed than what you offer on LinkedIn, for example. Also, you will find yourself often communicating with a variety of customers–from disgruntled to excited–and must be capable of getting a clear and engaging message across without expressing ire.

For all areas of marketing, you must demonstrate an understanding and ability to Copywrite. This means you are capable of writing advertising texts that will increase brand awareness to new customers and inspire greater brand loyalty among existing customers. Your copywriting skills must include the ability to write clear, concise, and engaging content that will compel sales or educate the masses, depending on the company's goals.

Because your work consists of advertising, another desirable skill is design, such as graphics design and videos. According to research provided by the courses and articles provided by Canva's Design School, consumers develop greater engagement when images are provided, and they garner more demand when videos are included. While plain text satisfies a share of customers, the numbers show more consumers respond more favorably when visuals are included.

The final two necessary additions to your resume that will be mentioned are proof of analytical and budgeting skills. The required analytical skill is broader than what is required of other careers. In this case, your understanding of analytics for social media metrics such as likes, comments, and shares–and general business metrics–such as website traffic, leads, the conversion rate from leads, and revenue–will be tested. Expert digital marketers are capable of tying both metrics together to gain a wider understanding of how the company's image is viewed, what needs to be improved, and how to better engage the target audiences. These metrics are also used to determine the effectiveness of your social media marketing strategies in meeting the business goals.

As for your budgeting skills, you may find yourself allotted a budget per advertising project. Your ability to juggle the expenses of designs, images, analytical tools, and management tools for social media will be tested as you work to improve the brand's image within the budget's constraints. Proving to have basic budgeting and financial knowledge is generally enough for some companies to consider your resume.

Active and Passive Marketing

Assuming your interest in becoming a social media marketer has not waned, determining the difference between active and passive marketing can help you decide whether you should make a self-employed career or dedicate your time to an established company. At the beginning of the chapter, it was mentioned that social media marketing could be active or passive, depending on your choice.

From what you have read about what is needed to pad your resume to prove you are an expert social media marketer, you can see that this is an especially active approach to making money online. It will be a full-time job, and if that is what you are looking for because you are not content with your current work, then this is a fair career to get into. That said, if you are not looking for a career change and are instead looking for a boost in your income, then taking a more passive approach to digital marketing is the direction you want.

Passive marketing is ideal for those people who lack time to dedicate themselves to actively engage with audiences. The low effort of passive social media marketing consists of creating content for easy distribution among the chosen social media platforms managing the calendar for when content is distributed, letting the content draw in viewers who will potentially convert, and answering questions and comments when necessary.

Passive social media marketing is the utilization of analytics, marketing, and promotional tools that are designed to advertise your product or service with little or no supervision. These tools consist of but are not limited to, ad campaigns on Google or Facebook, Search Engine Marketing (SEM), and Social media Marketing (SMM). As an expert social media marketer, it is up to you to make these tools generate the traffic and sales that will boost your income.

The ads speak for themselves: They will pop up on websites as potential customers browse the Internet and entice the viewers to click on the ad. Depending on how you set up the ad, you could make money just from viewers following the ad, or you can make money when the viewer converts into a buyer. The SEM and SMM are tools used to monitor activity.

These tools assist digital marketers in finding their target audiences and tweaking the advertisements to better influence viewers. The catch is using such tools is the price for having them. Certain sites will offer limited features for free, such as Audiense, which is a platform that assists digital marketers in managing their Twitter marketing and analyzes how their marketing is received by the targeted audience.

The free features are extremely limited and basic. Typically, they are not enough to get the feel you need for what your audience is interested in and whether you hit the mark, so it is common for marketers to pay the premium prices to improve their marketing abilities. This explains why budgeting skills are important for social media marketers. The prices for Audiense, for example, range from $79 to $696 a month if you choose to buy an annual subscription, or can range from $99 to $1,499 a month if you choose to subscribe month-to-month.

This is where the difference between actively and passively e-marketing shows. You need the tools provided by sites like Audiense regardless but can better generate sales by being active. Being active allows you to interact with the audience like Amazon's marketers and influence their decisions with subtle marketing through those interactions. The better your engagement, the greater likelihood of converting viewers into buyers.

Active marketing also allows you to direct your customers' engagement. You can call your viewers and encourage them to visit your brand or the company's brand by marketing contests, encouraging them to stay connected by following the company's Twitter, Facebook, or Instagram accounts, and gauge the generated traffic at the same time. Being active improves your chances of receiving feedback from surveys too, which further improves your marketing abilities because you will gain valuable information about what the customers are thinking and interested in based on their responses.

Starting Your Social Media Marketing

Becoming a social media marketer for an established company can be difficult when you have no experience to prove your abilities. Without connections, cold pitches, and follow-ups to ensure the company at least looks at your submitted resume, the likelihood of landing a career with the company is slim at best. That is why most people choose to build their brand and digitally market their newly made business. Regardless of your choice, you must be familiar with how to work as a digital marketer.

To begin your social media marketing career, you must first plan your marketing strategy. This strategy will be the summary of what you hope to achieve, how you hope to achieve it, and will be the guide for your success. The best strategy to design is concise, reasonable, and specific. While it is good to dream big, it is important to have attainable, reasonable goals in mind when building your strategy. Social media marketing is still a career or secondary source of income. It must be treated with the realistic expectations you would have about your day job.

Work S.M.A.R.T.

So, when you choose your strategy's goals, it is recommended you create S.M.A.R.T. goals that are achievable and align with the objectives of the business or your brand. The acronym stands for "specific, measurable, attainable, relevant, and time-bound." S.M.A.R.T. goals are used by professional digital marketers to determine whether their actions lead to the desired result and measure their return on investment (ROI).

The "specific" in the framework is just that: Be clear about what you are trying to achieve and ensure the progress of attaining this goal is trackable. Do you want to gain X number of followers, or do you want to convert X number of viewers into buyers? Be as specific as possible, so you do not lose focus.

The "measurable" is the metric you use to gauge your success or failure. In the case of improving follower count, your metric could be like this: First, determine your baseline followers (how many followers you started with) and identify the percentile increase of followers within an established timeframe. This allows you to determine your progress in achieving your goal of improving follower count.

The "attainable" is your social media goals that seem just out of reach but can be achieved when you put in the required work. This means your goals should be challenging, but not impossible if you set the correct pace for achievement. Here, you will determine whether your specific goals meet the attainable requirements.

The "relevant" guideline is used to determine whether your set goals tie back into the purpose of the company you work for, or for your business. The goals must make sense in how they benefit the company or your business, so deciding you want more followers to "like" your posts on Facebook or Instagram, ensure there is a relevant reason for why this benefits the company or your business.

Finally, the "time-oriented" guideline keeps you accountable. This is the timeframe for completing the set goals to provide timely check-ins on the progress of your success. Typically, milestones will be added to the timeline as reminders of how you are progressing.

Know Your Audience

With your strategy made, your next step is to learn about your target audience. Who will benefit from the product or service you are offering? What do they want to see or interact with on social media? You must know the content that will grab your chosen audience's attention, keep it, and compel them to do business with the company or your brand.

When determining the interests of your audience, you should know specific information such as the age range, the general location, interests, and average income. Information from these categories allows you to determine whether your audience is susceptible to purchasing based on impulse, desire, or need. You will also have a better understanding of how best to communicate with your audiences and where.

For example, despite the popular belief of Baby Boomers (the generation born between 1946 and 1964) flocking to Facebook and outnumbering other generations, the truth reveals how Millennials (those born between 1981 and 1996) still greatly outnumber them in usage. This reveals the stereotype assumptions should not be trusted over the analytical tools used to measure social media usage. Were you to make use of this information; then you would likely determine Facebook as a strong lead for placing ads directed toward Millennials instead of Boomers, thus adjusting your budget to accommodate these changes and potentially save on your budget.

Watch Your Competition

Just as knowing your audience is crucial, knowing your competition and how they are faring will also improve your marketing chances. Observing how they engage with customers on social media and whether it is working to vitalize their sales will provide insight into what works in the industry you have chosen. You also learn what works, what does not work, and how to recognize when your social media marketing is well-received by your audience.

Watching how and where your competition focuses their digital marketing efforts can provide you insight on where your competition is lacking. For instance, you might realize that your biggest competitor has impressive activity on Facebook but is severely lacking on Instagram. This can be used as an opportunity to dominate on Instagram rather than struggle to compete on Facebook.

Must-Know Tips on Marketing

When keeping tabs on your competition, you may find setting up a social media management tool designed to monitor relevant keywords and accounts in real-time help. Programs like Hootsuite allow you to insert information about your competition so you can always know what they are up to, how they are doing, and how their audience is responding to their activity.

You can also use this to audit your social media presence. This is especially important because it will make discovering fake accounts easier. As your brand's presence grows in popularity, you will run into scammers who use your business name or product names to steal followers and customers. This is harmful to your brand and customers, so the ability to audit your brand's presence gives you the power to report those scams before they tarnish your reputation.

Because you will be marketing yourself on multiple social media platforms, you must remain consistent with your brand's identity. If you want the brand to be seen as fun and witty, ensure you incorporate fun and witty content on every platform you engage in. It will also help to have the avatar and username for each account to be consistent.

Your communication and writing skills will be crucial to your success as a social media marketer. You should always strive to learn and be better at both, so finding resources that will help you improve in both is important. For communication, you should consider attending TED

Talks about communication. These are often run by inspiring speakers who are considered experts in their field.

As for your writing, you can improve it by broadening your vocabulary and brushing up on popular terms used by your audience. Following Merriam-Webster's Twitter can up your vocabulary game. Not a day goes by without their Twitter making snarky comments about misused and made-up words, so watching their feed can be a great warning for what not to say in your content.

After some time of posting content in hopes of gaining more sales, you will find your list of ideas dwindling. Creativity is crucial to being a successful digital marketer, so keeping your list sprawling with ideas will keep your customers engaged and your sales soaring. To keep the creative ink flowing, consider attending online communities or classes designed to inspire you.

LinkedIn Learning is a good start when searching for classes and services to teach you how to change up your writing or image placements. Joining a community like Creative Mornings can connect you with leaders in marketing and design, so having successful individuals like that in your circle will ensure you never run out of ideas.

The Pros and Cons of Social Media Marketing

Like all ventures, there are considerable ups and downs in choosing social media marketing as your online money maker. The pros and cons of being a digital marketer depend on which route you take: Will you be a freelance e-marketer, a direct-hire for a company, or run your brand?

If you are a freelancer or market your brand, one of the greatest pros is the profit. As a freelancer, companies are often willing to pay upwards in the thousands to get the best social media marketing available. At the same time, when you run a business or brand, you can market everything yourself and save those thousands by cutting out the middleman. Both prospects mean big profits for you. As a direct-hire, the company gets the bulk of the profit while paying you a stable wage and possibly offering bonuses for jobs done well.

Another pro to being a freelancer or marketing your brand is the schedule you work. You are the boss, so you determine whether you will work that week or if you will work a couple of days. Freelancers make the terms and can either stay firm about it or compromise with the client. Marketing your brand gives all the power to you, so you never stress about having someone breathing down your neck about getting the job done, unlike being a direct hire.

As mentioned before, companies are always looking for social media marketers. If you choose to freelance or work directly for a business, you will find yourself always in demand by the companies, small businesses, and solo entrepreneurs who need to outsource the marketing tasks. This is not as useful if you choose to market your business yourself, but it can be good to keep in mind if you choose to redirect your attention and need someone to continue e-marketing your brand.

To balance the positives of being an expert digital marketer, you will find the negatives are equally compelling. For one, not all companies understand the value of having social media marketing experts. You will be hard-pressed to sell the benefits of engaging on social media and why you would know best on the matter.

When you do finally get the client to work with you on social media marketing, you will then be constricted by their needs. Your ability to take on the client's tone, beliefs, and attitude will be tested as you engage with their audience. Be aware that they may be looking for formal, clear-cut conversations with the masses. If you prefer engaging customers with fun and upbeat content, then you must familiarize yourself with the social media accounts connected to the business to determine whether you are a good fit.

Being bound to a company's expectations–both as direct hire and as a freelance digital marketer–also means adhering to their policies, algorithms, and other standards for social media marketing. It will be your responsibility to always be aware of any changes to their standards and requirements. While a direct-hire may be informed in meetings and by fellow employees, freelancers may require inquiries or hope their HR team remembers to speak with them.

A major drawback to being a social media marketer is the blur between your professional and personal use of the platforms. You may get so used to being on Instagram or Twitter for marketing that you forget to stay professional on the business account or forget to relax on your private account.

An example of this is when McDonald's digital marketer made the mistake of inserting personal feelings and political interests on Twitter. In that instance, the e-marketer voiced political displeasure while also insulting the person tagged in the Tweet. It was a bad day for McDonald's and that e-marketer. For social media marketers, it was a day to never forget because that demonstrated the backlash of mixing your career with your life.

A final drawback to consider is the risk you take when posting content. Your message must be clear and have no chance of an ulterior interpretation. Otherwise, backlash and outrage will ring across the Internet for years to come because even one person misunderstood the intent of your message.

This is what happened to Dove and its social media marketer at some point. Negligence of how the audience would interpret the ad caused a wave of confusion and disapproval from the masses. The targeted audience did not interpret the message as it was meant to be understood: That Dove offers products for these specified women. Instead, it seemed the women were changed as if the product altered their very race upon use.

It was a terrible mix-up and caused grief for the company for some time, and the digital marketer who originally proposed the idea is most likely employed elsewhere after that disaster. Learn from that mistake and ensure you understand every possible implication of your content's message before displaying it for the world to see. The message must be undeniably clear for your sake and the company you represent.

This is especially important if you are marketing the products or services of your business, too, because then you will be tasked to address the masses over the backlash while also unable to "let go" of the digital marketer who made a mistake. You will do yourself a disservice if you consider for even a moment that your message is clear enough and does not require review.

CHAPTER 4
Conquering Retail Arbitrage

Social media marketing can be a stressful choice for making money online and has many requirements that may seem like too much effort for an income boost or new career. If this is an issue you dislike, then perhaps retail arbitraging is the venture you want. It requires you to be more physically active than digital marketing, but the activity is inherently easy because it can be done when you planned to go shopping at Walmart, Target, or wherever, anyway.

The idea of retail arbitrage is straightforward and easy to get started in. The practice of this business module has you purchasing goods at any retail store you planned to visit anyway, and then selling those goods for-profit online. People who practice this business often flock to the clearance section of stores to guarantee their profit margin. The goal is to acquire as many discounted items as possible so you can sell them for full price or if you feel confident about the inflated price.

A common question about this line of business is whether this is genuinely profitable. In many cases, it is, but only because these cases have people who have done their research and are aware of what is in demand and how much you spent to provide it to online customers. You must also consider the price of shipping and any fees that come with placing them on certain marketplace platforms.

The more you can buy at once, the better your arbitrage business will fare, and the more profit you will immediately make. The only catch is having somewhere to sell everything you gathered. Most people practicing this business choose to sell on well-known marketplace platforms like Amazon, eBay, or Facebook's Marketplace.

You may wonder how this is any different from regular retail, which purchases the stock at bulk for discounted prices and then sells to the public. The difference is that individuals are going to physical, brick-and-mortar retail stores to find products to sell. So, say you were looking through Walmart's clearance aisle, and you noticed stacks of all-purpose bandanas were discounted to $1.00 each from the normal $1.75. Someone practicing retail arbitrage would eagerly snatch the stacks to purchase.

These stacks would then be sold somewhere like Amazon for a profit. They might choose to sell at the set retail value of $1.75 each, or they might aim for greater profit by selling them at $2.00 each. Either way, they will have made a considerable profit if the bandanas sell well.

For someone hoping to make easy money online but being new to the concept, practicing retail arbitrage is a good start. It can net you enough money to grow more confident in pursuing other avenues, such as dropshipping or the broader spectrum of e-commerce, or it can become your preferred money-making method. This is especially preferred by those who do not have the desire to create their businesses online.

Retail Arbitrage in Action

As mentioned a few times now, people practicing retail arbitrage often flock to sites like Amazon, eBay, and Facebook. Of the three platforms, Amazon has always been the most popular. To this day, Amazon continues to be relatively lenient about retail arbitrage and does not have policies that police anything is sold by resellers. There are a handful of categories that are "gated," which means proof of invoices from the manufacturer or distributor must be provided to sell these items.

For Amazon, this list includes, but is not limited to, jewelry, major appliances, and gift cards. There are also times when other categories that are not typically included in the list will be gated due to the seasons. These categories are usually the games and toys due to big holiday swings like Christmas.

Retail arbitrage is run similarly on eBay, though the people on eBay like to consider themselves experts on the products they purchase and sell. This is because they have chosen to focus on products that they are especially familiar with, such as shoes for people with wider feet. Having a specific category that you are most familiar with is called a niche market. This is a smaller segment of a larger category that is defined by specific parameters, such as knowing the value of collectible coins.

An example of this is how someone might focus on purchasing video games at a discount and then flipping them for profit because they know the full value of the games is still high. Others may be especially familiar with biking gear and know that the bike wheelset they just purchased for $150.00 is easily worth $300.00 with the right buyer. So, of course, they will want to make that easy profit by putting it back up on sale once they have it.

When practicing retail arbitrage on Facebook's Marketplace, it has become common practice to scour the "free" section for gold mines. Assuming you have a niche category that you plan to sell in because it is something you can easily gauge the value in, the "free" section in Marketplace is an ideal place to search for those diamonds in the rough. Once you have the item or items you want to sell and know the right price that will net you a profit, you can either post what you have on the Marketplace or turn to Facebook groups to further enhance your chances of making a solid sale.

Another practice with Facebook's Marketplace is finding the deeply discounted items there, then turning around to sell on Amazon or eBay for the intended profit of full price or inflated. Some practitioners of retail arbitrage do prefer Facebook's Marketplace over other sites because unlike Amazon and eBay, for instance, Facebook does not charge you a marketplace fee for selling through them. Regardless of where they choose to sell, though, their profit is guaranteed so long as they know how to attract the right customers.

What You Need to Know When First Starting

When starting your venture with retail arbitrage, it is generally recommended you have a niche to call yours. While you could go out and scavenge every clearance aisle of every retail store local to you, not knowing the fair value and whether it is a popular item will get in the way of making a genuine profit. This is why researching one or two niche markets and making them your expertise is ideal.

For example, if you are an individual who loves working on vehicles, you may be ready to dig deeper and find niche markets involving vehicles. You could become an expert on tires of all makes, sizes, and life expectancy. Tires are always up for sale on eBay, Facebook, and Amazon. With your specific knowledge on tires, you could take advantage of those posts selling tires at supreme discounts and make a profit on them.

Another way to make use of niche markets is by toying with how else the item may be accepted. For example, if you have a collection of antique plates and glasses that are gold- or silver-plated because you found them in an open house that was giving everything away for free, you might be tempted to put them up in the "Home and Kitchen" category of your chosen marketplace platform. If you know the value of these plates and glasses, however, you could put them in the "Collectibles and Fine Art" category because the set you snagged might be a collection from a famous brand.

Once your niche markets are chosen, your next step is learning how to use keywords to your advantage. The keywords are what draw your prospective audience to your posted sales. The more relevant keywords you can include in your posted item's page, the greater chances of finding an interested buyer and making that profitable sale.

Having an image or set of images to further advertise your available stock is also highly recommended. When conducting sales, buyers will always look closely at the shared pictures to determine whether the price matches the real value, or if there are any telltale signs that what you have is a knockoff of the desired item. You will know the truth of your item, so make the images serve the purpose of getting your stock sold.

Alongside this is being an expert at writing descriptions. For sites like eBay and Facebook's Marketplace, the description will also be a key factor in whether that viewer converts into a buyer. Adding descriptions to aid viewers in finding your product will improve the chances of selling stock. Furthermore, having descriptions to further promote the key selling factors of your stock will essentially guarantee a sale.

In certain cases, you might even consider using your expertise in the niche markets to determine what sorts of misspellings people would search when looking for your products. For example, someone could mistakenly type "camra" instead of the proper "camera" in their haste. If you are familiar enough with your niche market to know the potential misspellings, you could be crafty by adding common misspellings in the descriptions or titles alongside the proper spellings for your products. This way, you will still attract every aspect of your targeted audience.

Must-Knows for Retail Arbitrage

Though Amazon, eBay, and Facebook's Marketplace are all highly popular sites to park your arbitrage business in, know that there are other options available too. You might have friends or friends-of-friends who are interested in something you found at a discounted price. Take the example with the tires: You might have found a set of tires that were made in the 36th week of last year and verified that the condition is nearly perfect due to little use. Your friend mentions she knows a guy who is looking for tires to fit his truck because the tires that came with it were mud tires, and every truck person knows mud tires will get torn up on the paved roads.

Because you are always scouting for the best deals on tires, you know that you have just the tires for the guy, so your friend arranges a meeting for the tires. He knows the value of the tires almost as well as you do, but he does not know how much you paid to get them. You offer to sell them at a "discounted" price from full retail value because he is a friend-of-a-friend and the guy, knowing this is a deal he should not miss, happily accepts. Just like that, you have performed a version of retail arbitrage and made the desired profit. The opportunity to sell your stock is everywhere, so long as you are looking. Do not blind yourself by sticking to the typical three platforms.

When making your sales, a general rule of thumb is to sell your product for at least 3x the price you purchased from. While it is possible to make a profit on anything by just upping the price by a few dollars at a time, you will never make enough of a profit to make an effort worth your time and miles on your car. This is also why you should have a niche market or two under your belt. Knowing a ballpark estimate of what you are looking at makes it easier to determine whether you can make a profit of at least 3x what you paid.

If you prefer the safety of selling on familiar sites, then selling on Amazon will make determining potential stock easier. Amazon has a free app that you can download on your phone to help you make smart buying decisions. It is a scanning app that will scan the barcode of what you are looking at and informs you with a glance at how much that item is being sold on Amazon, how much is taken out by marketplace fees, and the total of what you can expect to earn in the end.

Legalities with Retail Arbitrage

A major question often asked about retail arbitrage is whether this is a legal practice. The short answer is "yes," this is legal on all accounts. This practice is not like price gouging, which is the practice of deceptive or unfair trade practices during times of disaster, such as the global pandemic of 2020. Price gouging is illegal in the United States, and getting caught has several ramifications, including imprisonment for a year, a fine up to $10,000, and being banned from ever selling on certain marketplace platforms again.

Retail arbitraging does not have such extremes because, again, it is considered legal. It has already been addressed in the US Supreme Court as a venture that retailers cannot prevent because the merchandise the individual is selling is, as proven by the receipt, legally purchased by the retailer. This means the purchased merchandise is yours to do as you please, and if reselling it is your plan, then you are legally allowed to resell it.

With this confronted and proven legal on the US Supreme Court level, the best way to protect yourself from any false accusations from retailers is to keep every receipt involving purchases that you plan to turn into stock for your retail arbitrage venture. Any attempt to challenge your right to resell your legally purchased merchandise should not stress you because your receipt is the only proof and permission needed to continue your business. There are certain challenges you may want to consider, however.

For one, trying to sell merchandise from brand names can result in harassment from the brands. They do not appreciate retail arbitraging and will do everything in their power to intimidate you into ceasing your reselling venture. You are once again reminded that there is nothing to be legally done against you, which is why the best these brands will do is harass and intimidate. You have every right to resell the merchandise you bought, and they have no power to stop you.

Despite the legal protections you have in reselling your purchased merchandise, be aware that the sites you choose to do business on may choose to be stricter than the laws. Your seller account will be under constant scrutiny on the marketplace platform, so if there is ever a complaint about the legitimacy or quality of your product, the platform's rules may favor the customer's view because a receipt from the retailer does not prove the authenticity of your product.

Finally, as far as legal matters go, it is often recommended to consider your retail arbitrage business as a temporary means to make money online because of how easy it is to lose your good standing with the marketplace platforms. It is argued that this should be a means for getting accustomed to learning how the e-commerce world works. This is especially the case when the harassment, intimidation, and potential challenges from brand names eventually make a successful argument against your practices that leave you with only the option to agree to refrain from reselling their products.

Pros and Cons of Retail Arbitrage

The ups and downs of choosing to make money through retail arbitraging are as extensive as those of being a social media marketer, but one of the pluses that can beat out the latter is the price to get started. Because you do not need a monthly subscription to get started and stay active, it is debated that retail arbitrage is a lower cost venture to start. Whatever money you have on hand should be enough to pick up a few items in the clearance aisle of whichever store you happen to visit.

Because it is as easy as browsing the clearance aisle and picking up a few items to get started, retail arbitrage is considered to have a low barrier to entry. It is exceptionally easy to find a Walmart or Target to browse, and if you were going to the store anyway for other reasons, then it could be considered a "fun" addition to the trip because you will be looking at items you normally would not consider.

The ability to resell everything is also relatively simple. It takes just a few minutes to set up a seller's account on Amazon or eBay, and there is even less effort needed for Facebook's Marketplace because everyone has a Facebook account to start. This ease of reselling everything is made better when you consider how little marketing investment will be needed to get people to want your merchandise.

This is because the items you choose to sell will already have an established presence in the retail world. Your only role in the marketing process is getting your stock posted onto the marketplace platform with relevant keywords that will get your product noticed by customers who are already searching for what you are offering.

The downsides, however, include the harassment and intimidation tactics that you will likely face when trying to sell brand items. If you are not mindful of the quality of your products and unable to brush off their attacks, continuing your retail arbitrage will be difficult. Not all marketplace platforms will protect you, but if you do sell on a platform that offers some form of protection, do not be surprised if the brands find a way to circumvent those protections to get into your head.

Another major downfall to running a retail arbitrage business is the lack of control for profit margins. When running a business that sells products or services, the desire to get the most for your money will always be strong, but that desire cannot always be met with retail arbitraging. This is because what you spend is dependent on whether a retailer has your desired merchandise on clearance, and because the profit you earn back will be against the price plus the marketplace's established fees.

Finally, retail arbitraging is time-consuming. If you want to make extreme profits from this venture, you find yourself needing to bounce between various retail stores in town to find goods that are worth reselling. Then, once you have all the stock you can get, it will all take up space in your home while you wait for customers to find your posts and purchase from you. Only then are you able to run to the postal office and send the merchandise on its way, which means another trip filled with running around town

CHAPTER 5
Dropshipping Success To Your Door

Throughout the book so far, you have seen the phrase "dropshipping" repeatedly used with little to no context. You know that it is a means to make money online, and it is relevant to e-commerce and retail. Simply put, dropshipping is a mostly self-efficient online retail fulfillment store. A dropshipping store does not have products physically cluttering your surroundings or forcing you to rent a warehouse to hold everything. Instead of you physically holding the desired products, everything is held by a third party, like the original manufacturer or an established wholesaler for the product. Your store is the middleman for the customer and promises the customer they will receive their purchase while having the third party handle the shipping.

By being the middleman between customer and third party, you are rewarded a cut of the profit because your store is what drew the customer to the product. Many successful drop shippers claim this is an easy means to make money, but they warn that this is not a scheme that gets you rich quick. The success stories like to say it is easy to start and that you will make money in no time, but they skip the finer details about dropshipping.

For one, it will take time to create a successful dropshipping business because getting started can be a difficult task when you do not know how to begin. You must know what tools are best, find websites that allow dropshipping if you do not want to create a personal website, and know the trends for what sells well. This online business requires you to do the necessary research about what people are looking for and to know which companies are willing to partner with drop shippers.

Despite the rough start that many will face, know that running a dropshipping business is worth the effort. It does not require you to dedicate every moment of your day to it when starting. You can take your time to learn how it works and set it up when you have time. Once it is up and running, your efforts will be rewarded in a few ways.

For one, it requires little to no supervision to run. So long as you keep up with the trends and update your stock occasionally to meet those trends, your dropshipping business will run itself. This venture is also a solid choice for receiving passive income.

Dropshipping is a simple and sustainable business model that allows you to control it from anywhere in the world. It is also considered one of the ideal ways of making money online. Entrepreneurs and anyone looking to boost their income especially appreciate that it requires little hassle and money to start it.

Pros and Cons of Dropshipping

Like any daring choice when attempting to make money online, choosing to build a dropshipping business has its pros and cons. A pro to dropshipping is how easy it is to get started. You do not need any experience in running a business to get started, and you do not need any form of inventory either. In that sense, this business model has the retail arbitrage beat because no need for inventory and social media marketing beat because no need for extensive knowledge or research.

To get started, you just need time to learn the basics and set everything up. You will want tools to make the business run smoother on its own, but they will not be necessary for the beginning when you are starting. If you choose not to worry about the tools in the beginning, then starting your dropshipping business could be as easy as starting today and having it ready to run within a few hours.

Once started, it will be easy to grow your business, which is saying a lot when compared to retail arbitrage. The model for your business will not change by much as you grow your stock to match demand. The only difference would be how much effort and time you put into marketing and making sales.

You have the option of changing nothing and letting your business handle itself how it always has, but upping your participation even by just 30 minutes a day for more marketing will make your business grow faster and more lucrative. That is a small downside if you are hoping for an entirely passive income. This business model does require you to put in small bouts of effort to ensure you draw traffic to your store.

Other than having to market your store here and there, the dropshipping business is among the easiest businesses to manage. This is especially the case because the model is designed to run itself soon as you find a supplier for your store. Your customers will order what they want, and your suppliers will take care of the rest. Your only worry is getting traffic for your store.

With your supervision being so minimal in the equation, you will find dropshipping to be one of the most flexible avenues available for someone looking to make money online. You set the rules because you are the boss, and since this is a passive income, your rules could very well state that you work once a week, and you would still make great money from it.

This flexibility also extends to where you want to work. Because it is entirely digital, you can check on your store from anywhere that has Internet. You can also do this by phone if you do not have your laptop readily available. The best part is having it running even when you choose to take vacations with family or friends. Also, when you are struck by inspiration or discover a trend you never expected, you can adjust your store on the fly because it is that flexible. So, if you find a product that you want to test, you can easily add it to your store and see how it does. If it does not work out, then it is equally easy to remove and move on.

Finally, one of the most appealing pros to starting the dropshipping business is the minimal demand for money to start. Technically, you can get started without investing a cent in the business. Managing to start without spending anything will require quite a bit of work on your part, however, because that involves hunting for free trials and starter plans. Choosing to go the completely free route will also affect the quality of your products, so you should weigh whether saving money or providing high quality is more important.

The Cons to Dropshipping

Bear in mind, for every pro to dropshipping; there is a con to consider. The level of competition, for example, is a considerable con to weigh. Because the barrier to creating a dropshipping business is so low, the number of others flocking to this idea will be considerable. It can be difficult to make your store stand out if you find three others that are not just selling similar products but are selling the very same products as you. Speaking of products, one of the risks you take with not personally handling the inventory is the lack of control pertaining to it. When you do not see the product before it ships to the eager customer, you cannot know for certain whether the product is of high quality. Other than purchasing an item yourself, you are stuck, relying solely on customer satisfaction and feedback.

Your customer satisfaction is crucial and will be affected by every problem caused by suppliers. For example, if you have multiple suppliers attached to your dropshipping store, your customer may suffer the displeasure of multiple packages being delivered from different brands. This can cause the quality of your products to vary wildly and may cause confusion because of the different branding.

With so many variables involving your product, maintaining a positive customer service experience will be especially challenging. Your suppliers' failures will reflect poorly on you, not them, so the pressure will be on you to assuage your customers' ire. The blame is entirely yours when mistakes happen on your suppliers' part, and you must be ready to accept your customers' complaints on your suppliers' behalf.

A major setback to choosing the dropshipping business is the initial profit margins. In the beginning, suppliers will not be impressed with your decision to start this business because, as mentioned, there is stiff competition for you. The fees and priority will be a hurdle at the beginning of your venture. This can change when you develop a reputable storefront because then you can negotiate exclusives with suppliers, but until you reach that point, the profits you make will not be substantial.

Dropshipping in Action

For many people who have chosen to make money online, the pros of dropshipping far outweigh the cons. The flexibility is a dream come true for many people who work a day job, and they have nothing to lose if customers get upset because they will still meet their bills regardless of the dropshipping store's success. These people consider this business model a side hustle.

The most they sacrifice to make this store run is a few minutes of their day. Also, dropshipping is a model that rarely gets labeled as a conflict of interest. This opens the door to working online for many people. If you are among the few who happen to work a sales position, it is still recommended you speak with HR about the company's non-competition policies to ensure there is no conflict of interest.

Treating the dropshipping store as a side hustle is especially ideal for those people who often work overtime for their day jobs. It is a struggle to juggle a work-life balance as it is, so adding a side hustle can skew the balance worse if you need to put hours into it. This enforces why dropshipping is so favored. As stated previously, you do not need to invest much time to do your dropshipping business work because it will essentially run itself once it is set up.

There are many cases where dropshipping has become a full-time day job because it has grown large enough to become a reliable source of income. The best part about turning your dropshipping store into your full-time job is learning how to turn the previously unstable income into a steadier stream. It will be relatively unstable as a side hustle because you will not have the time to perfect it, but that makes your ability to turn this into a career even more impressive. However, this route requires more work on your part. Luckily, you do not have to throw yourself into the process to make it happen. You can start it as a small side hustle and work your way up at your own pace.

The people who transformed their side hustles into full-time jobs are those who developed an effective marketing strategy to draw in customers, figured out how to use the trending interests to their advantage, and learned how to dropship efficiently. A full-time drop shipper will have a business model that works like clockwork and generates passive income even as you sleep.

If you choose to build your dropshipping business into a full-time job after getting used to it, you may eventually decide to tackle another side hustle. This is a common step for well-established drop shippers because the business model is so flexible and runs so well with minimal supervision. Full-time drop shippers do not spend eight or more hours every day on the store, so they have the time to establish another successful source of income. If that is something that interests you, then dropshipping may be the business model for you.

Starting Your Dropship Business

When getting started, the first step is deciding how you want to establish your store. The most common tactic is to choose an established online marketplace like Amazon or Shopify and then set up shop. The particularly ambitious individuals may go the extra mile to build a standalone website for this venture.

As a beginner, it is recommended to start with the online marketplaces you are familiar with, then grow from there. It may be exciting to build a website and have it be your storefront, but it is also time-consuming and requires the know-how of coding the website to run properly. You will also need to put together graphics designs for your website, including backgrounds, banners, and logos for your self-established website. If you are unfamiliar with these background skills, it will cost you quite a bit up front.

Play it smart and debate setting up the fancy website for when you choose to go full-time. For now, choose an online marketplace you know for your shop. Most people choose to work on Amazon, eBay, Etsy, or Shopify. If you know of other marketplaces that offer equally lucrative opportunities, then feel free to start there instead.

Once you have your marketplace chosen, you must then consider the following: what you want to sell, what suppliers are willing to work with you to sell that product, and how to get your sales tax ID.

Deciding what you will sell is the most crucial step in setting up. Like what was explained in retail arbitrage, you will want to establish a niche market to dropship in. The more specific your niche market, the better your chances of establishing your store as a reputable source for the product become. This is a step that you must take your time researching on.

There is this belief that you can dropship in any niche market and become successful. This is a half-truth. You technically can succeed in any market, but you will encounter staggering competition if you choose to compete in a niche market that is already oversaturated by other drop shippers or major brands.

When choosing your niche market, base your decision on personal interests and hobbies. Your unique knowledge on the products will further establish your reputation as a source of desired products because you could get into the finer details of the interest or hobby. For example, you may find yourself running into a consistent problem with a product because it regularly requires a small fix to make it more durable. That experience can lead you to turn the small fix into your niche market, thus allowing you to become an established source for others who suffer the same issue.

Before settling on that niche market, however, be sure to do your research. See how many stores or brands also offer that product you want to sell. This is to determine whether your market is overly competitive, reasonably competitive, or essentially barren. If your niche appears barren, you should follow this with determining whether the product is genuinely profitable. The general rule of thumb for determining profitability is ensuring your margin makes at least 40% after all the necessary fees are taken out.

Another factor to consider with your niche market is the size and weight of your product. Successful dropshippers will insist you focus on the smaller and lighter products when first starting. This is because you must consider the cost of shipping, which increases based on weight and size. After you have gained traction as a reputable store, you can consider whether selling larger products is worth it based on any deals you make with your suppliers.

Successful dropshippers also insist on the best range for making a profit is anywhere between $15 to $200. This is once again aimed at beginner dropshippers because this price range is easier to manage when starting out. You are free to change your products and prices as you grow more comfortable running your dropshipping business.

Once your niche market is established, the next step is to find your supplier. This is also a process that requires time and research because not every supplier is friendly to dropshipping. You must do your research and make contact when necessary to ensure you are establishing connections with the right suppliers for your store.

You should look for how much experience the supplier has with dropshipping and whether the sales representatives you speak with are genuinely helpful and informed about the business model. The better and more detailed their answers are, the more confident you can be about choosing to partner with them.

Do not waste your time with a supplier that you feel lacks experience with dropshipping. If you feel the sales representatives are only as knowledgeable as you or less, then you are likely to struggle with this supplier if you choose to partner with them. Remember, your store is the middleman between customers and suppliers, so you suffer any complaints the customers have because of supplier mistakes.

One of the most important questions you must ask the sales representative involves the fees for orders. You can expect your supplier to always have a fee for packaging and shipping on your behalf because they are holding the available inventory and doing the majority of the work for you. The typical fees you will pay run a few dollars, roughly around $5. If the supplier you speak with wants to charge more than that, then it is best to politely turn that supplier down and move on. Spending any more than that cuts too much into your profit margin to be worth your time.

Another important question to pose to the sales representative is whether they can provide referrals. Experienced suppliers for dropshipping businesses will have connections to similar businesses, so this should be no problem for the supplier to offer. These referrals will verify the supplier's dropshipping experience and provide a feel for customer satisfaction.

Finally: the sales tax ID. Certain suppliers will not work with you if you do not have a sales tax ID before speaking with him, so it is recommended to invest in this before contacting suppliers. This is required by every state excluding Alaska, Delaware, Montana, New Hampshire, and Oregon. It is relatively inexpensive to apply for your tax ID, but it may be a process that is just as time-consuming as the previously mentioned steps. This is because you may be required to establish yourself as a business entity and have a Federal Tax ID number before you can acquire the sales tax ID.

Services and Tools for Optimal Dropshipping

After you have established your niche product, acquired a supplier, and settled on the marketplace you want to start on, the task of acquiring tools to best optimize your dropshipping business will be next. This is particularly necessary if you want the business to run itself. Most tools you will find can plug directly into your business, so you will have easy access to everything from the dashboard of your business.

The downside to acquiring tools for your business is the price that comes with each tool. Like the tools for previously mentioned business ventures, these often require monthly subscriptions. A few tools offer starter plans for free, but the best quality of these tools is guaranteed to be locked behind the most expensive plans. It is up to you to determine what works well enough and where you need to spend.

A popular tool to acquire is one that gives you access to verified dropship suppliers. Tools like Oberlo for Shopify or SaleHoo are well-known for their databases and directories. SaleHoo is especially popular because it offers annual subscriptions or a one-time purchase, whereas Oberlo has plans that range from $30 to $80 per month. SaleHoo is generally the recommended tool when searching for suppliers.

If you want to save time putting together your inventory, tools like Inventory Source are best. These tools can cut your labor by automatically placing the order to the supplier when a customer purchases a product on your website. Inventory Source offers its services for a minimum of $50 a month.

When keeping track of trends, you can rely on services like Google Trends to update you on what consumers are looking for every day. It is good to keep track of what consumers are most interested in, but also keep track of what products are not as widely desired. You may discover a profitable niche that you would not have otherwise considered.

Other tools and services available for tracking the market include Google Keyword Planner and the "best sellers" sections of websites. The Google

Keyword Planner is a good addition to your list of tools and services. By typing in the name of your product, you can learn how often your product is searched. It is recommended you establish a niche that is searched at least a few thousand times every month. Using the "best sellers" sections of online marketplaces and other websites will help provide an idea of which niche markets offer the most traffic and which markets customers are particularly unhappy with.

CHAPTER 6
Life With E-Commerce

While learning about the potential money-making business available online, you have seen the phrase, "e-commerce" repeatedly mentioned without explanation about what it is and how it is relevant. E-commerce is the shorthand for "electronic commerce," which is the business model that allows businesses and individuals to sell or buy desired products and services online. E-commerce is the digital shopping experience everyone enjoys from the comforts of their computers, phones, and tablets. For many people, e-commerce has become the preferred means of shopping. This explains why retail arbitrage and dropshipping have become successful over the years. The ability to find almost everything you want by scouring the Internet has made the online earning potential lucrative. If you follow the statistics for e-commerce, you will see that its popularity has steadily gained traction with an exponential upward curve. By choosing to join the e-commerce world, you are opening the door to immense possibilities for profit.

When debating whether to pursue an income through e-commerce, you must be aware of the types of e-commerce available. First is the business-to-consumer, which is the most basic model. This consists of selling products or services to customers, like selling a phone case to a customer with a new phone. The next is business-to-business, which consists of offering goods or services that will assist a fellow business in its own pursuits. An example of this would be selling copy machines or payroll software for the business to utilize.

There is also consumer-to-consumer, which is like private sales. An example of this is selling your couch on eBay or Facebook's Marketplace because you are moving. The fourth and final type of e-commerce model is consumer-to-business. In this instance, the consumer could be a photographer offering his or her licensed photos to a business.

It is more common for individuals hoping to make money online to fall under business-to-consumer or consumer-to-consumer. The consumer-to-consumer is more likely if this is meant to be a boost in income and remains as a side hustle. For those who strive to do this as their full-time job, business-to-consumer is the goal.

The Differences Between Dropshipping and E-Commerce

There may be questions about the difference between dropshipping and e-commerce. The first difference is the objective of the two business models. Dropshipping is focused on marketing your store's specific goods to convert viewers into consumers. The products provided by dropshipping businesses are also held and shipped by the suppliers, who are third parties to the dropshipping businesses.

E-commerce is the digital version of a brick-and-mortar retail store. These businesses have all the inventory they are selling and are not limited to specific suppliers the way dropshipping businesses are limited. Individuals or businesses running an e-commerce model are also more detailed about their market research, and they are more active about maintaining inventory levels. This ties into the larger difference between the two models: Dropshipping can be automated, so it becomes passive income, whereas e-commerce qualifies solely as active income.

The cost of starting each business model is also vastly skewed. With e-commerce, you must purchase the stock from wholesalers or manufacturers like how retail arbitraging goes to physical stores to obtain stock. Also, like retail arbitraging, e-commerce must have somewhere to store this stock, which leads to the business renting buildings for storing everything. These costs rapidly add up in the beginning, making it difficult to get started. This is not the case for dropshipping, as explained in the previous chapter, because there is no stock for the dropshipping entrepreneur to physically handle.

Another difference between the two models is the profit margin. Dropshipping is limited due to the relation with suppliers and established longevity. The newer the dropshipping store, the less will be made compared to the fees of the marketplace it is established on, the fees from the supplier—or suppliers if the store is partnered with multiple—and the shipping costs. E-commerce businesses have a greater opportunity for profit because the research they put into customer interest is translated into bulk purchases of the desired product. This allows them to reduce spent money and maximize profits.

Finally, the ability to maintain positive customer satisfaction is greater for an e-commerce business than a dropshipping one. This is because the e-commerce business controls the flow of products, further ensuring a quality product is swiftly shipped to the waiting customers. Services for the customers can be customized to their needs, too, like personalizing the packaging.

Dropshipping businesses are solely reliant on the third party's standards. This reliance puts the dropshipping businesses on the unsteady ground with the customers because they cannot guarantee the demanded quality. This is especially problematic when the dropshipping business has multiple suppliers. Customers may grow frustrated with receiving packages from different sources at different times with varying quality.

Launching your E-Commerce Business

Launching your e-commerce business is similar in how you would launch a dropshipping business. To begin, you must choose what product or service you want to sell. You should consider what you are knowledgeable about, whether it is something that has consumer demand, and whether there is significant competition selling it. You should expect to spend considerable time researching and analyzing viable product ideas before researching how you will obtain your chosen product.

Depending on your product, your options for supply would be making it yourself, contacting a supplier, or contacting a manufacturer. The choices for your supply can be one of two: domestic or overseas. There are pros and cons to both, so you must consider whether the pros outweigh the cons of your choice.

For domestic, the primary pro is the higher quality you can expect for your products. The result of this, however, is the con of high manufacturing costs. As for choosing an overseas source, the reverse can often be said. The manufacturing costs are significantly lowered, but often at the cost of the product's quality.

With your product chosen and a supplier acquired, your next step will be to write out your business plan. This plan is meant to keep your goals focused and ideas relevant. It will also be your guidelines for effectively attracting new customers and turning viewers into consumers.

Your business plan should be an evaluation of your idea, have clear phases or goals put in place, and strategies that you can immediately use. It will give you an idea of how much work must be put in to make this successful and be a gauge of what you can expect, budget-wise.

After you have completed the above steps, you must then consider the details of your business. For example, what is the brand name of your business? It must be appropriate and relevant to what you are selling, but cannot infringe on the copyrights of other businesses. It is also best to work out a business name that can be used in the domain name of your website.

You must then consider your brand's logo. Every business has a logo that helps consumers immediately recognize the business. When first starting, your logo does not have to be fancy. Keeping it simple makes it easier for you to move forward with the business. You can always improve the logo after you have become an established e-commerce business.

Next will be the task of building your online store. You will start by choosing an e-commerce platform. This platform is a software that allows you to manage your website and business, including marketing and sales. Most beginners will resort to products that help build e-commerce websites because creating a website from scratch requires coding and graphics knowledge that is not common for the average consumer.

One of the largest available platforms is BigCommerce. It offers search engine optimization (SEO) tools that will help your store be noticed whenever consumers search for products or services and are easy to customize. This site does not immediately say how much it will cost to use the services, but you can expect to pay roughly $29.95 a month for the standard business plan.

Another platform to consider is WooCommerce. This is considered ideal for starter stores and anyone looking to expand into the e-commerce industry. One of the perks it offers is making sales tax easier to understand and completely removes the guesswork when starting your e-commerce venture. Its business plans are free, but that also means the platform is limited in what it can offer.

There are many platforms available to choose from, so do your research to find one that best suits your needs. Once you have chosen the platform to start your business, you will set up your store. The platform you choose should help walk you through this step. When you complete this, you will be ready to launch your store and join the e-commerce competition.

Tools for Optimizing Your E-Commerce Business

Like the previously explained online businesses, tools are essential to running a successful e-commerce business. You will want analytics, business, customer service, and marketing tools to help propel your business to exponential growth. Also, like the tools explained in previous chapters, you can expect to pay monthly subscriptions for what you choose to use here.

For your analytics, you may want to start with Google Analytics. It is free to start and has everything you may need when running your business. Google Analytics will assist you with understanding how people experience your site, determine how well your business is performing, and offer detailed reports on important information. This includes the conversion rates from viewer to buyer, traffic flow on your site, and reports on how well your advertisements are attracting your targeted audience.

Google does offer an advanced version of Google Analytics called Analytics 360, but the price tag on the advanced analytical tool is steep. It costs $150,000 a year to use it, which is why everyone from newcomers to medium-sized businesses chooses to settle with Google Analytics. As interesting and potentially useful the locked features may be, you will find that Google Analytics already offers plenty of insight to successfully grow your business.

Another analytical tool you can consider is KISSmetrics, though it will cost a minimum of $299 a month as of this writing. This tool will help you grow your e-commerce business by providing compelling data about your customers. It will provide reports on who your best customers are, where they come from, and how to convert viewers who are like your best customers. You will also learn where your business is going wrong with customers based on traffic source, viewer profiles, and what is dissuading viewers from becoming buyers.

For your business needs, consider trying the Kit tool. This will help with your marketing needs by providing you a virtual employee to set up and manage social media accounts. Your virtual employee can create a Facebook or Instagram for you, post store updates, and provide email marketing campaigns on your store's behalf. A word of caution if choosing to use Kit: The price is based on the ads they run on Facebook or Instagram for you, so it will be difficult to say what your monthly bill is unless you research how the ads work.

Another viable tool for your business is Wiser, which is an intelligence tool that monitors your competition's prices. This allows you to optimize your products' prices to further scale and grow your business. Finding the price on this requires you to undergo a consultation with their sales representatives, so this may be highly selective.

If you find customer service daunting, then consider acquiring tools or services that will handle them for you. Try Smile.io, which is a tool that boosts customer loyalty to your brand by building a loyalty program. You can use this to reward your customers with points whenever they make purchases, share their purchases on social media, or refer others to shop on your site. The starting price for this tool is $49 a month and climbs as high as $500 a month.

You can also use Yotpo to garner more customer reviews that will improve your sales with relevant feedback. Yotpo is particularly useful because it can be automated to send emails requesting reviews or surveys to customers who recently purchased products from your site. You can request a demo to test the waters or jump into it and create a free account to get a better feel for the program.

Pros and Cons of the E-Commerce Market

The pros and cons of e-commerce do overlap with what dropshipping has to offer. For example, you can expect customers to explore your store late at night while you are sleeping, and you can expect to make money while you are away from the computer. One of the pros that stands out is the freedom to sell internationally. By targeting audiences outside of your home country, you open yourself to global competition and can become a successful demand in the global market. Also, depending on the currency conversion, you may find yourself earning more by selling overseas compared to domestic.

A more popular pro is how personalized you can make the online shopping experience for your customers. Personalized home pages can really sell your site to potential customers. When you know the interests and trends of your targeted audience, you can adjust the website accordingly to properly appeal to this audience and entice them to shop around. An adjustment you can make is adding relevant content that entertains and entices your viewers to convert into buyers.

With a properly personalized store, you can make it especially easy for your customers to find the products they want, making this experience worth repeating in the future. You can also take advantage of what your data analytic tools report by including well-placed ads that guess at what your customer may have missed while shopping, or adding clever bundles based on the customer's behavior on the site.

As your store grows in popularity and traffic, you will find the ability to rapidly scale your business promising. As your earnings increase, your budget to advertise and stock up on products will increase based on demand. Depending on how much time you are able to dedicate to your e-commerce business, you can easily make this your career and live comfortably from a successful business.

Cons of the E-Commerce Market

As exciting as e-commerce may sound, bear in mind the drawbacks to it as well. One such drawback is when your site crashes or is down for maintenance. You cannot earn when no one is able to reach your store, so it is crucial you do your research on what platform to host your website on.

Another drawback is the competition. As a startup business, you may find yourself against stiff competition, which appears to be dominating the niche you have chosen. If you are stubborn enough to struggle against the competition, you may strike gold and grow in popularity with enough time, but it is difficult and can be a discouraging venture. This emphasizes the importance of researching your product ideas. Your best bet will be targeting a different audience. Otherwise, study your competition's marketing strategy to see where they lack so you can dominate that strategy instead.

A major drawback involves customers. As an e-commerce business, you will not have sales representatives at the ready for any questions your customers may pose. Because most people are impatient for instant gratification, you can lose a customer faster than replace one. Delayed responses are bad for your business, so find ways to get around this struggle. Utilizing a chatbot or hiring customer service representatives can help, but it depends on your budget.

Finally, one of the worst disadvantages of running an e-commerce business is shipping. Customers dislike having to wait long periods for their product and may demand faster shipping. While it is possible for you to meet the demand, it will cost you a premium to make it happen for them. There is no perfect resolution for this because someone will have to make an unwanted sacrifice. All you can do is be transparent about the shipping times and hope the customers do not leave the checkout screen empty-handed.

What Not to Do in E-Commerce

Because you are new to e-commerce, you have a convenient opportunity to learn from others' mistakes. A common mistake people make is choosing an e-commerce platform that is not compatible with the user's needs. It cannot be stressed enough but *research* the platform before you settle on it. Every platform offers unique tools and services, but not every tool or service is beneficial to you despite how appealing it all sounds.

The platform you choose will determine how your products are displayed for the digital world, and it will determine who all will find you. You must be aware of how much control the platform allows you to customize your store and attract customers. You should also be mindful of the experience your customers will have when arriving at your store. If it looks cluttered or is difficult to navigate for your customers, you will lose out on sales.

Another issue you may run into is the cost of your platform. This cost is not in reference to the monthly subscription to the platform, but the cost to your ability to grow. If the platform limits your business in any way that you find crucial, then your business will struggle to grow into something lucrative.

For example, choosing a platform incompatible with your vision can lead to the critical mistake of spending money on a platform that you may ultimately abandon. This is a devastating setback for anyone trying to make money online, regardless of whether you have a day job to cover the expenses. It will be a waste of your money, time, and effort. This is especially the case when you consider how much you spend to migrate the store to another platform that has its own monthly subscription to contend with.

Other mistakes your predecessors have made include not targeting a specific audience. They will have the website and supply set up brilliantly, but suddenly realize they lack conversion from viewer to buyer because they did not define the audience they wish to target. Correcting this mistake requires extensive market research, and this defines why your predecessors may have struggled.

After all the research and analysis conducted just to start, the need to research the market interest of their audience is often swept under the rug by the assumption that consumers will come because you have what they want. While it is true that the audience will find the desired product, that does not guarantee they will find the product on your website. The audience is more likely to choose a store that has marketed the product as a solution to their needs in a way that resonates the best.

To not fall for the same mistake predecessors have made, ensure you understand what values are important to the audience. Learn what language your audience uses so you can tweak the SEO in their favor. This teaches you how to better communicate the pros of your product to your designated audience and enhances your ability to stand out from the crowd of competition.

A major mistake your predecessors are likely to have made is failing to make a lasting impression. Your product can be top of the line and revolutionary, but if your store lacks a strong message or identity, no one will think twice about looking at your product. Your products can make a strong impression you want once they are in the consumer's hands, but your brand must make a strong impression to get your products to the consumers.

There is a reason why Starbucks, Nike, or Samsung are so well-known, and it is because they have brand messages and identities that stand out from the rest. People see their logos and immediately recognize them. You hear their brand names and immediately know what products and services they offer. Be like these successful brands and stand out.

Finally, make sure the checkout process is not complicated to utilize for your customers. This is the step that makes interested consumers close the tab to your store. Customers are looking for the gratification of an easy purchase for something they want or need. If your checkout process is complicated with unnecessary obstacles like pop-up ads encouraging them to buy more, then you are likely to permanently lose their business. This translates into poor customer service and transforms into poor customer feedback. You will never know how many people that customer has influenced and convinced to never shop on your site, and for no better reason than the checkout process was inconvenient. For a customer, inconvenience can take many forms.

One such form is being forced to create an account before being allowed to check out. Obstacles are nuisances, especially if the customer has already spent too much time searching for the product in the first place. If the customer wants to create an account, then you can expect a new account to be made without you having to push them to make it.

Also, it is recommended to not hide any terms or fees from your customers. Hidden terms and fees are regularly taken with negative reception, so be upfront and honest about what your customers can expect. Have it clearly listed out in the checkout process and offer a means for them to see more details if they desire.

CHAPTER 7
You Can Blog

A blog is a website featuring commentary and niche information. Blogging is a popular means of making money online because it is considered fun for many users. It is also considered an innovative source by businesses for marketing while also being a great source of income by itself.

There are many directions you can go with a blog. If you were to search for anything on the Internet, you are guaranteed to find blog websites that have insights to share about the information you searched. Blogs are all over the Internet, and new blogs continue to spring up every day because it is such a popular avenue for making money online.

Most blogs are written with informal, friendly tones and offer commentary like what you might read from a diary. These are typically personal blogs run by individuals who are looking to share their interests or experiences for the benefit of others. You can also find more formally written websites that are directed toward more serious subjects, like politics or technical purposes.

You can expect blogs to have very specific niches to discuss, though there are a few that choose to touch upon many subjects with no discernable preference. The popular niches include sports, travel, smartphone technology, and opinion pieces about politics. Despite how saturated such subjects may be, it is still possible to get noticed and earn a decent income.

Your goal when starting a blog is quite simple: You plan to share valuable information that your viewer wants to know. If you are running a business, like e-commerce or dropshipping, having a blog is a good way to advertise your products, too. In the case of advertising for your side business, your goal would be to draw as many viewers as possible by ranking high in the search engine. The more traffic generated on the blog, the greater potential of viewers converting into buyers for your side business.

Running a blog alongside your business can also connect you with your customers. Your blog can be used to keep everyone updated about any changes you plan to make, provide exclusive deals to those who keep up with the blog and garner customer interaction to better understand their demands and needs. You can also make the blog more informal and personalized, so the viewers develop a stronger connection with you and your brand, garnering greater customer loyalty.

That does not mean blogging is meant to only supplement other online business ventures. Blogging by itself can be a lucrative means to earn money. Take the blog, Gizmodo, for instance. This website was launched in 2002 and has grown in popularity and recognition since then.

Gizmodo is particularly known for discussing designs and technology but does occasionally dabble in other niches like politics or science.

This blog grew exponentially with these established niches and was able to turn into a global endeavor. Now, Gizmodo has secondary websites dedicated to translating the content into French, German, Spanish, and other languages. At the time of this writing, it is known that Gizmodo earns $325,000 every month.

Another well-known blog is the Huffington Post. This was started in 2005 and has since grown into a wildly popular source for liberal commentary on life and politics. The creator of this site, Huffington herself, made quite the name for herself with just a few years of dedication. Though she eventually sold it to AOL in 2011 and stepped away from writing, there is no doubt she made a killing in her time. To this day, AOL continues to reap the rewards for investing in Huffington Post to the tune of $14,000,000 every month.

Sites and Tools for Optimizing Your Blog

As you can see, running a blog has genuinely unlimited potential. The trick to acquiring such potential is utilizing the right sites and tools on your blog. Both Gizmodo and the Huffington Post made the most of their blogs' space by utilizing advertisements.

For example, Gizmodo liked to use ads that repeatedly appeared as you scroll through the blog's content. Whenever you changed pages, a new repeating ad would appear, and the cycle would continue. Huffington Post also used digital ads, but these ads were not repetitive in the same sense. Instead, the banners and other ads used on Huffington Post were all sponsored, meaning the revenue was even greater whenever someone chose to follow the ads and links.

The tools both sites utilized are what helped them make such enviable income. One site that can help your blog succeed is Quora. This may come as a surprise, but the reason this is a fair start to your blogging career is that it is a website dedicated to answering questions.

Blogs are meant to provide meaningfully and desired information to their viewers, so what better way to learn what your viewers want to know than going to a website where you can find their questions? Using Quora will help you brainstorm the topics and niches you want to delve into. It is also easy to use because you need only to type in keywords that are relevant to your blog, and you will immediately be brought to a page with questions about your keywords.

If you are like most writers and struggle with creating a compelling title, then consider the Portent Title Maker tool. It will randomly generate a title and clever breakdowns of how to make the title an interesting and relevant read. This can also be used to brainstorm content ideas when you are running low on inspiration after searching your keywords on Quora for a while.

Organize Your Thoughts

Once you have ideas, it is best to find a way to organize them all, so your content does not jump around and confuse your readers. Consider organizing your thoughts with Trello or Evernote. Both are particularly popular choices because they can be used for everyday needs, like grocery shopping lists or quick reminders of sudden additions to your day's schedule.

Both choices are easy to organize and make it simple to sort through your jotted thoughts. Evernote is especially popular because it allows you to tag your recorded ideas. You can use that tagging feature to further emphasize your idea with reminders of tone, the date you want to publish it, whether you want to add photos, and other important information that would not fit in the note.

You might also want to use a calendar. This is to help you keep a schedule for your blog posts without you overbooking your day, week, or month with too many ideas. When you feel inspired, add your idea to the calendar, then look over the entire month to make sure you do not have too much slotted for one timeframe. This will become a common problem, so keep your calendar close to avoid overbooking your time.

Optimize Your Content with Keywords

Much like the e-commerce and other business models, utilizing a Google product can be considered a must. Google Trends is the ideal product for blogging because this will let you know whether your brilliant idea for a blogpost is popular enough to make public. This is a keyword search engine that gives you an idea of what consumers are looking into.

An equally convenient tool is Google's Keyword Planner. While Google Trends is used to gauge the popularity of your idea, Keyword Planner is meant to provide you details on what popular words have the most search volume. It will also provide related keywords to your search to broaden your chances of garnering viewers. This can be used to inspire you for your next blog post.

If you choose to use the popular blog platform, WordPress, you should consider taking advantage of SEO plugins. These are designed to fine-tune your content to include keywords and phrases that are popular in the search engine. Certain plugins like Yoast SEO will give you an idea of the best placement for SEO keywords or phrases, then provide a green light when it has determined you ready to publish the piece.

And Up Your Blogging Speed

Finally, tools that will increase your writing speed and make your writing easier to consume. First would be utilizing a timer, such as Egg Timer. Your efforts will be timed in increments of your choice in an effort to improve your speeds. This tool is a free website that allows you to type in the desired timeframe you want to work and then hit Start.

Most bloggers set the timer to allow them 15 minutes to conduct necessary research, 40 minutes to write the initial draft, and so on and so forth. It might seem far fetched, but timing yourself and keeping tabs of how much you accomplish between each count down will improve your writing speeds.

You can also use a tool called Toggl. Where Egg Timer is a simple tool meant to time your speed, Toggl allows you to time yourself and see the stats of how you did. This tool offers you a dashboard with information revealing where you spend the most time and what you need to work on. You find this particularly useful if you are curious about how long research takes you compared to writing and editing the content.

To improve the quality of your writing with minimal effort, consider using the Hemingway tool. This is a free marketing tool that will assess and offer input on your writing. It goes as far as highlighting sentences to emphasize what it recommends changing and explains what is wrong with the sentence. It also informs you of the readability level for the piece, allowing you to adjust when needed if you feel the reading level is too high, like technical, or too low, like sixth-grade level.

Grammarly is another popular tool for improving your writing. It has a free, premium, and business plan for users, but it is generally acceptable to use the free plan. Bear in mind; however, the free plan is extremely basic about its sentence structures, punctuation, and the like. If you find it vetoing your comma placements despite you knowing that a comma is fine to use, then try upgrading to premium. You may find premium accepts that comma's placement despite basic's insistence.

Visually Stun Your Audience

Finally, you must consider tools that will improve the blog's appearance. There are many photography platforms available with stock photos available for you to use. The trick is finding visuals that fit your needs. As mentioned earlier in the book, you can use sites like Shutterstock to find stock photos relevant to your blog posts.

Another good source for high-resolution photos would be Death to the Stock Photo. This website is owned by artists who have dedicated their time to providing consumers unlimited downloads of their stock photos. Death to the Stock Photo offers two plans: Free, which is email only, and premium, which allows you to freely browse their stock photos and build a personal library.

If you are uncertain about Death to the Stock Photo, then start with the free service. You will receive an email every month with links to a collection of free stock photos. These links will be the extent of your access to their collection, but that should be enough to provide an idea of whether the site is for you.

Other than using stock photos, you can also use image tools to create visuals for your blog. Consider using Canva or Gimp to create images that would better fit your theme or visuals. Canva is particularly popular because it comes with premade templates that you can transform into unique visuals for your blog. Gimp is a free version of Photoshop. It is recommended to use Gimp if you are familiar or have time to create fancier graphic designs without the use of premade templates.

Starting Your Blog

The start of your blog will be like the start of the previous business models: Find your niche market–or, in this case, your niche topic. When it comes to blogging, it legitimately feels as if the sky's the limit. If you are passionate about gardening, then there is an audience waiting to hear from you. If it is traveling, fashion, games, or even just providing reviews on anything under the sun, then there is an eager audience waiting for you to share what you know.

When you choose your niche topic, make it something you are passionate about, so you can enjoy it as much as your viewers will. The only requirement for your topic is to ensure you have an audience who wants to hear about it. You may be able to spin any passion into a viable topic if you are creative, though, so go wild with your list of ideas.

With a list established, the next step will be validating which topics will work out. Like with e-commerce, you want to gauge the competition levels, observe how your competition approaches the subject, and determine whether there is potential to earn an income on the idea. If everything checks out, then you are ready to run with an idea.

Your chosen topic will also influence the name of your blog, so be mindful of what you settle on.

Once your topic and blog title are established, the next step will be choosing the platform to host your blog. Most beginners choose to use a well-established blogging platform like Medium or WordPress, and this is viable. WordPress is considered the number one hosted platform for blogging and is used by many successful blogs. The drawbacks are the limitations stipulated by the platforms, but as a beginner, it can be a stepping stone worth testing.

These platforms are usually free and have a subdomain attached to your URL to show that you are utilizing their platform. This can be detracting to your credibility in your blogging career, but when getting started, this may be a sacrifice worth making. Another important consideration when choosing to utilize hosted platforms is the ownership of your blog.

If you are not self-hosted, then the hosted platform is the "real" owner of your blog despite you running it. This is because the blog's domain name is attached to someone else's "property," so if that platform decided your blog was breaking terms of service, your blog would run the risk of being deleted. This is more common than bloggers realize, so be mindful of what you are signing onto.

This is not a problem when you are self-hosted. The domain name is no longer attached to another platform, meaning it is entirely yours. There are no terms of services that can be used against you because the blog is now on your online property. So, once you are more comfortable with blogging, it is recommended you immediately transfer into a self-hosted platform. You will have a domain name to call yours, and there will be no restrictions on how you run your blog. You will, however, pay a few dollars a month to own that domain name. $5 to $10 a month is a small price to pay to ensure your blog cannot be deleted by someone else, though.

With your platform and domain name decided on, you are now ready to design your blog. Assuming you chose to start with a hosted platform, you will have access to premade themes by the platform. Feel free to decorate the blog as you see fit, but be mindful of your blogging goal as you decorate. Remember that you will have consumers viewing your blog searching for content relevant to their interests, so keep the navigation simple to prevent frustration and loss of traffic.

When you finish designing your blog, you must then consider how you will monetize the blog. There are three established ways of generating income through blogging. First, you can provide informational products. These are online courses, e-books, et cetera designed to provide detailed information that will help consumers accomplish their goals. For example, if you are knowledgeable on woodworking and staining wood, you could provide courses that detail the different types of woodworking and the best ways to stain wood.

Next: freelancing and consulting. This means turning your blog into your selling point by showing potential clients your ability to write cohesive and concise content that draws in readers. Social media marketers may utilize a blog to showcase their skills by writing witty conversations with customers. Freelance writers might turn their blog into a portfolio that demonstrates their mastery of the written language to prove their value to prospective clients.

Finally, you can use affiliate programs to make money. This is done by strategically placing ads on your blogs, like Gizmodo and Huffington Post. They found brands to partner with and were clever about promoting the products from their partnered brands. Depending on the type of advertisement chosen, you can earn either by the number of clicks on the ad or by the sales of a product from someone who followed your advertisement.

Building your blog with affiliate programs is the simplest way of generating an income. This is accomplished by attracting large and steady traffic to your blog to increase your odds of consumers following your established links, and then subtly promoting your partnered brands either by placing ads on the sides of the blog or by discussing the brands' products in your content.

Once you have decided on your means of monetizing the blog, remember to include your blogging tools before officially launching your blog. With everything in place, you are ready to start writing content for your blog and building an audience. Remember to have content ready for your blog's debut, and to have a steady schedule for publishing more content. The more consistent your blog is the better chances of customers consistently returning to see what you have to say.

Pros and Cons of Running a Blog

The best part about using a blog as your online money-making venture is how easy it is to start one. You find something you want to talk about, hop onto a hosted platform if you do not want to go through the hassle of establishing an official platform, and you start posting content. This genuinely makes the entire experience sound easy and fun.

Also, the earning potential is ludicrous. The means to make money is straightforward if you choose to use affiliate marketing. You just talk about the products of the brands you affiliated with, set a few ads around the blog, and talk customers' ears off about subjects they want to know.

Another benefit of blogging is that it costs little to nothing to get started. You will also learn what works and what does not as you go along, making it stress-free when getting started. There are virtually no barriers to getting started, thanks to the low startup costs. This means you can experiment and play around with your blog as much as it takes to establish the tone and image you like.

One of the most exciting pros to blogging is engaging with your audience. You can attract consumers from around the world and influence their daily decisions with your content. Connecting with people from other countries and walks of life will broaden your horizons and open your eyes to more possibilities. Such experiences can also turn into blogpost material if you are creative.

Cons of Running a Blog

However, there are downsides to consider when blogging. First and foremost is the time it takes to run the blog. For example, the content will not write itself. You must take the time to research, draft, edit, and submit based on your publishing schedule. You will also throw your time into analyzing keywords and phrases to ensure you are still relevant to your audience's interests.

This is not to mention the potential interactions you may want to hold with your audience in the comments section or the interactions you may entertain with fellow bloggers. Genuine work goes into blogging, so you must be prepared to dedicate the necessary time to make this work. This includes finding a way to regularly update the blog.

If you have a full-time day job while you are blogging, then you should expect your patience to be tested with this venture. Keeping a schedule for blogging on top of your day job's schedule will be draining, so your patience and persistence will be truly tested as you strive to make this work. Success will be slow at the beginning with your limited availability. This will reflect in your blog's traffic level as it starts from zero and works its way up. The time it takes to grow into something impressive may feel draining, and it will be worsened when you realize that this is not a get-rich scheme. The money you make in the beginning will feel like a joke because it will be so small, but it will be a start. With enough patience and persistence, you will see that amount steadily climb.

Finally, you must be mindful of how you handle your blog. As traffic becomes steady on your blog, you will find people starting to recognize your blog as an established and reputable source for information. This means you must be careful of what you write, how you write it, and how it will reflect on you.

This will be a business that earns you income, so do not mix your personal feelings with your content. Like the example made in the chapter about social media marketing, do not repeat the mistake made by the digital marketer for McDonald's. Be aware of how you present yourself online, so you do not accidentally tarnish the reputation you worked so hard to establish.

CHAPTER 8
Connections In Affiliate Marketing

Affiliate marketing was touched on during the chapter about blogging as a method to make money while blogging. You do not have to rely solely on blogs to make affiliate marketing work for you. Affiliate marketing is an online means to generate sales by partnering with others who are targeting the same or similar audiences like you. This partnership allows you to earn a commission whenever you send a paying customer to your partner's product.

To make this business model work, you must be dedicated and persistent because affiliate marketing rewards you based on performance. That performance is how well you convert viewers into buyers for your partners. It is popular to attach affiliate marketing to blogs, but it can also be used on social media platforms or personal websites. Your personal websites could be other business models that you have started, such as dropshipping or e-commerce. Of the mentioned models, bloggers are considered to have it easier.

Blogs are meant to draw high volumes of traffic just because they have niche information to share. Adding a few relevant affiliate marketing ads or links to the content is easy. Also, because the viewers are there for the specific information in the first place, the desire to purchase based on the provided information is organically higher, thus providing a convenient and easy segue to converting viewers into buyers.

This common business model is utilized in many industries. For example, it is common to find influencers participating in affiliate marketing. Influencers are the equivalent to online celebrities. They use the influence gained through their fame to persuade their masses of followers to follow the ads or links to affiliated merchants and make purchases. For influencers, affiliate marketing is extremely lucrative and easy money.

There are three ways to earn an income with affiliate marketing. First, you have the standard model called pay-per-sale strategy (PPS). This model has merchants paying the affiliate (you) a percentage or commission for helping convert viewers into consumers. This is typically done by redirecting viewers from your website to the merchant's page.

Next is the pay-per-lead strategy (PPL). With this program, you will be sending viewers to the merchant's page still. Instead of being paid when a sale is made, you will be paid when the viewer decides to sign up for programs, products, or services with the merchant. The sign-ups can be for anything, from joining the merchant's mailing list to trying a trial. The terms are dependent on the agreement between you and the merchant.

This strategy is more lucrative than the standard PPS because it is typically easier to get someone to sign up for deals and free trials than it is to convince that same person to make a purchase. It is especially successful if you regularly receive high traffic on your site and know how to redirect your audience to see what the merchant is offering.

The third affiliate marketing strategy is pay-per-click (PPC). This program rewards you each time a viewer clicks on the link or ad that leads to the affiliated merchant. Once again, if you receive high traffic on your site, then this strategy can be particularly rewarding when you redirect viewers.

Myths about Affiliate Marketing

There are several myths about this business model that must be addressed before you consider whether this is the money-making venture for you. First, it is neither quick nor easy to manage. If you make this your side hustle while continuing your day job and expect it to be an easy hour or so of work, then you will quickly burn out from trying to make this work. Affiliate marketing requires extensive work, especially when you are competing with an oversaturated competition. The struggle will be that most situations are competitive, too.

There is a disillusioned belief that you need only to set up your site, choose someone to affiliate with, and let it roll out. If it was that easy, then everyone would be doing it, and bloggers would not need a publishing schedule to get their content recognized by the world. Affiliate marketing starts as an intensely active income, so you must be prepared to put in the necessary effort and time into it.

The effort and time you put into affiliate marketing will mainly be directed to fostering beneficial relationships with your partners to generate increased traffic on your website. For example, if you are running a dropshipping, e-commerce, or retail arbitrage business and have chosen to dip into affiliate marketing, you should have partners who are relevant to your business.

By guaranteeing their relevance, you should expect to increase your viewership *and* your sales. If the sales are not happening, however, then your partners are not efficient and must be replaced. You will find your time spent cycling through potential partnerships almost as often as having to update your content to inspire your viewers to make purchases.

Another popular myth about affiliate marketing is how to make the most money. It is inexplicably believed that the only way to make affiliate marketing work for your business is by being part of a market that is already popular and lucrative. This belief has led to many businesses choosing not to participate in affiliate marketing due to being in small niche markets.

Do not fall for this myth. If your niche market was too small, then there would not be a market for it. You should not feel pressured to break into larger niches just to reap the benefits of affiliate marketing. There will always be others you can affiliate within your market, and if you are creative, you may find yourself connecting with markets that can complement yours. It is fine to stay within the comforts of the niche, you know. Keep your business plan close and do not stray from your goals and progress because of this myth.

A third wildly popular myth claims affiliate marketing is a multi level marketing (MLM) pyramid scheme. This is blatantly false despite the charts, graphics, and what-have-you that may be attached to the claim. These exclamations are often punctuated with the expectation of affiliate marketing end, but there is no sight of such a thing. Affiliate marketing is not a pyramid scheme.

Pyramid schemes are illegal, but affiliate marketing is not. You also do not pay to start affiliate marketing, unlike MLM pyramid schemes. When you participate in an MLM pyramid scheme, you pay to have a product to sell without the product ever being distributed. Affiliate marketing bears no resemblance to such a scam.

Instead, it is like the dealers you encounter at dealerships when you shop for a new or used vehicle. The employee to help you purchase a vehicle gets a commission for the sale. Also, consider realtor agents. They get a commission for helping you purchase your home. Affiliate marketing is more like these examples, not MLM pyramid schemes.

The final myth that will be addressed is the belief that the affiliate marketing strategy is irrelevant to sales. This ties into the idea that the affiliate market is a scam and will end, but there is no verifiable evidence to support such claims. The belief stems from the ever-changing SEO algorithms.

These perpetually updating algorithms can make it difficult to keep your links active if you are not serious about affiliate marketing, but that does not mean the model is dead. Google and other search engines continue to find affiliate marketing as relevant resources for consumers despite the algorithm's frequent changes. There is no worry about affiliate marketing dying off anytime soon.

How to Affiliate Market

Getting started with your affiliate marketing business is relatively simple. To start, your affiliate marketing business requires you to already have a blog or website ready and in use. Having an established blog or website means you already have an industry or niche market, so that is one step done. Another step to check off the list is that you will already have products in mind or in place.

If you do not have a blog or website made already, then this will be the first step in starting your affiliate marketing venture. As you learned in previous chapters, you must create a domain name and decide whether you will use a self-host platform or use an established host platform. Once done, you must then just your industry or niche.

As previously stated, it is recommended to choose something that you are passionate about, as this makes it easier to stay committed to your money-making venture. While debating what industry and niche market to join, remember to research the viability of what is available. Consider what problems or needs you often run into in that industry or niche, then review whether that has potential as a sellable product.

With those steps done, the next step will be to research available affiliate programs. Doing the research is crucial, as this is the entire point of starting an affiliate marketing business. When debating which program or programs to join, consider the reviews from others who have joined, and whether the programs offer products that are genuinely relevant to your industry or niche. You might find yourself repeating this step several times because you should have multiple products in your industry or niche.

Experienced affiliate marketers recommend having only two or three programs. This is because it can become overwhelming to track your earnings from multiple sources, and it wastes your time when you have too many programs to search through for merchants who have products relevant to your blog or website. This becomes especially troubling if you choose to start scaling your affiliation business.

Once you have chosen the appropriate affiliate programs for your venture, the next step is tailoring your website's content to accommodate the ads and links. This will require you to be creative because there is no one-fits-all answer. Common methods of mixing the ads and links into your content are writing reviews on the products, creating tutorials on how to use the products, or simply inserting them into emails if you have a mailing list.

The final step to take is optimizing your website with the necessary tools that will detail whether your website is generating traffic, how to improve your visibility on search engines, and the overall engagement of your viewers. Once everything is set in place, you will be ready to throw your time and energy into becoming an affiliate marketing guru. Remember to stay vigilant about staying relevant, and to regularly research your audience's ever-changing interests.

Favored Programs and Sites for Affiliate Marketing

Among the many affiliate programs available, the Amazon Associates Program still tops the charts as a must-join. Beginners often flock to this program because everyone knows about Amazon. This popularity has influenced Amazon to create a beginner-friendly program that is easy to use and almost guarantees your application will be approved. The best feature of Amazon Associates is the list of available products for affiliation. You will have access to Amazon products and third-party sales.

Unfortunately, there are a couple of drawbacks to consider before leaping to it. For one, Amazon's terms are rarely set in stone, so you can expect these to change almost whimsically. The second drawback is how these changing terms affect your commission base. As of this writing, Amazon Associates' commission is not appealing. Unless you were already using or planning to use Amazon links on your website, this program may not generate much income.

The second most popular affiliate program is Awin. This marketing platform also offers a beginner-friendly experience and a significant variety of products for affiliation. It is considered one of the largest affiliate networks available despite its drawbacks. One such drawback is the application process for services. There have been complaints about it being time-consuming to acquire products and services for affiliations. As of this writing, the brands in this network often require you to create individual requests and sign-ups for the products and services you want. Another popular affiliate program includes ShareASale. Experienced affiliate marketers swear to this platform with their claims of greater commission values, competitive variety of affiliate products, and a genuinely useful customer support team. ShareASale is easy to join as the others mentioned and touts a reputation of longevity that cannot be argued against.

Recommended Tools for Optimizing Affiliate Marketing

In the affiliate marketing world, your greatest struggle will be maintaining steady traffic that arrives at your website, flows into your partnered merchants' websites, and becomes sales. To help you maintain this flow, consider learning from your competitors by using Ad Spy. Tools like this are designed to give you an idea of what designs your competitors are using, their conversion rates, and provide you with the best offers based on what the Ad Spy learned from watching your competitors.

Some consider AdPlexity a must-have for affiliate marketing. This is because it offers support for multiple traffic sources. It also provides you a means to find affiliates that offer the greatest profits. Experienced affiliate marketers claim this is essential if you are serious about affiliate marketing.

Another tool you want to consider is something to keep track of your affiliation projects. It is crucial to always know how well you are doing with your conversion rates. If you are unaware of where you stand, then you may never gain the traction needed to turn this business into a stable income.

Consider using RedTrack or AdsBridge. RedTrack makes it easy to see how your conversion rates are doing. It will show you the impressions, clicks, and conversions generated on your website. However, it does cost $28 a month just for the starter pack and jumps up to $939 a month for the enterprise plan, so you may want to test it before you consider making a purchase.

AdsBridge offers more advanced tracking tools but at the cost of simplicity. The monthly subscription for this program starts at $25 and climbs up to $595. Despite these prices, many consider its tools invaluable once you start scaling your affiliate marketing business.

One tool that every marketer must have is focused on mailing lists. Sending emails with ads and links to your affiliated partners is one of the easiest ways of generating impressions, clicks, and sales. Consider acquiring ThriveLeads and Constant Contact to make advertising via email easy.

ThriveLeads is particularly ideal if you are running your website from WordPress because you can use the plugin for it on WordPress. This email tool works to help increase the likelihood of viewers joining your mailing list, thus increasing your pool of potential converters when you send out the advertising emails.

Constant Contact is considered a one-stop-shop for your emailing needs. It makes it easy to manage your list of subscriptions. You can also have it personalize advertisement messages by sorting your subscribers. Finally, you can use Constant Contact to send the created emails, so you never have to juggle between pages to get everything sorted and sent.

Like what was described in previous chapters, you will want SEO tools. This includes Google Trends and Keyword Planner. Staying vigilant about what keywords and phrases are being used will always be a requirement when running a business online. There is no getting around their use. This is especially the case when you are trying to promote your affiliated merchants. If your audience is no longer interested in something you are affiliated with, then you need to know so you can make the appropriate adjustments on your website.

You want to always know what is trending in your industry or niche market so you can take advantage of that shift and stay relevant. You also want to keep up with your audience's interests. Understanding what keywords or phrases are most popular and effectively using them to boost your website's visibility is crucial in maintaining traffic, so do not slack in this department. If you are using WordPress, get the SEO plugins like Yoast.

Pro and Cons of Affiliate Marketing

When attached to other business models like blogging and the others mentioned in this book, affiliate marketing has attractive perks. One such perk is the passive income you can generate after enough work setting up your affiliate marketing model. Though you will be actively running it during the day to ensure you stay relevant and reliably redirect your viewers, your marketing will continue to run even as you sleep. It may not make as much compared to your waking hours, but income is still welcomed income.

Another welcomed perk to starting your affiliate marketing business is how low risk the venture is for you. Other than your time, it costs nothing to join an affiliate program. It is as simple as joining a program, setting up ads and links that redirect traffic to your new partners, and you get paid. It will be trial and error with each partner, especially when you are learning the ropes, but at least you lose no money for running into errors. A compelling advantage to affiliate marketing includes needing zero forms of customer support. As the affiliate, your job is to just get people from one site to the merchant's site. The products and services sold are not your responsibility, so any customer complaints will be on the merchant's hands. Your only participation in this is the step when you get paid commission for attracting the customers to your merchant partner. A personal favorite about affiliate marketing is the ability to work from home. The daily commute is not for everyone, no matter what time of day it is, and that plays a part in why working from home is attractive. You could also argue that you spend less money by going out and will rarely find yourself running late for work.

Running late for work is particularly nonexistent because of the convenience and flexibility affiliate marketing offers you. This can be considered a full-time job like the other business models detailed in previous chapters, so you become the boss of your schedule. If you wake up at 9 AM and want breakfast before you start marketing, then you can enjoy that breakfast stress-free because you still will not be late.

Finally, the most beloved advantage of affiliate marketing is the reward system. When you are a hard worker at your day job, your only reward is more work with little to no pay bump. That is not the case with affiliate marketing. This business model is performance-based, so your hard work will be rewarded well for the time and effort you put into redirecting traffic to your partners' products and services.

Cons of Affiliate Marketing

Unfortunately, there are several disadvantages to consider before making the leap to starting your affiliate marketing business. First and foremost, the hard work that comes with running it. Most people venturing to digital work to make money are not looking for a full-time job right from the start. Rather, it is both normal and recommended you continue your day job while you build your presence online.

The need to work hard, stay vigilant, and spend hours on this model can be draining after a long day of work. This makes affiliate marketing less appealing for the majority despite being among the most lucrative cash flows. It is highly recommended to dip into this model after you have established a different online business.

This disadvantage ties into another draining problem: The inconsistent cash flow. If you are running your affiliate marketing job on the side and hoping it will generate its fair share of income while you are busy elsewhere, then you will be disappointed by the inconsistencies of your side income. The inability to dedicate your days to this in the beginning stages will have you making very little, and at times, nothing.

Another tie-in to this inconsistent cash flow is that way you are rewarded. Affiliate marketing is purely commission based on your performance. While touted as a perk, it also doubles as a disadvantage because not everyone is interested in making another active income their career. There are people who just want to relax after years of hard work and still make a steady income. Affiliate marketing can eventually become that, but not before you put in the time and effort to grow it, then maintain a level of patience as you wait for it to become steady.

CONCLUSION

Thank you for making it through to the end of *Start Your Passive Income Business*. It was a long journey to learn about so many ways to make money online, so let us hope the book was satisfactory with its information. Hopefully, it was also able to provide you with all of the tools you need to achieve your goals in pursuing a means to make money online.

In this book, you have learned the difference between active and passive incomes, as well as the benefits of using both to turn a considerable profit. From there, the subjects evolved into beginner-friendly avenues of earning money online.

First, you learned how to turn your social media knowledge into a viable source of income. Marketing on social media can be fun, fulfilling, and extremely rewarding as a career. This job makes it so you can wow any user, and guarantee brand loyalty among customers with creative visuals and witty remarks.

Afterward, you discovered retail arbitraging is legitimate and surprisingly legal. It is an extremely active means of income and is not a 100% online venture, but it is beginner-friendly and easy to start. This was closely followed by dropshipping, which is a more passive avenue. When it comes to making money through sales, dropshipping is among the most highly recommended ventures for online businesses.

It is almost entirely automated, which gives you the freedom to spend your days; however, you want. Once it grows into a steady source of income, you can expect your days to be filled with enough free time to consider other interesting ventures. As explained in that chapter, dropshipping can easily bore you because it is so passive.

That is why some people prefer the level of involvement required in e-commerce. It is an active source of income, though it does offer the opportunity to become passive. The difficulties with this are similar to dropshipping but are far more rewarding in terms of earning potential.

Finally, you learned about blogging and affiliate marketing. Blogging is considered the easiest to get into, even compared to social media marketing, and arguably the most fun. It allows you to share your unique perspective and information with the world and opens the door to tying other online businesses together. With your blog, you can easily slip dropshipping or e-commerce links into the content, as well as affiliate products.

As for affiliate marketing, this is considered a more advanced business model due to it requiring you to have a blog or website to start. But this also means it offers the most lucrative means of cash flow of all. Though it requires the most time and energy, it is arguably the most rewarding business model you can start.

Now that you have these options laid out before you, the next step is to take the plunge and get started. Pick the business venture that appealed the most to you, return to the chapter so you can take advantage of the recommended tools, and take the plunge. You are fully equipped to start. The time is now.

Finally, if you found this book useful in any way, a review on Amazon is always appreciated!

DESCRIPTION

Working your day job can feel monotonous, tedious, and downright repetitive, even on the best days. Every day, you work hard to meet your quota. Some days your bosses are impressed and praise your work ethic. Most days, they dump more work on you with no offer for increased pay rates because you do the work so well already. It can be difficult to perform so well only to go unrecognized and unappreciated. You work day-in and day-out; for what? Minimum wage? A salary with an occasional bonus because the company did well that year? That is great, and all, but is it rewarding?

The thrill of making money wears off fast when you are bored because you know everything about your job. So, what if you dabble in something less familiar, like making money online? There, the possibilities are endless and, more importantly, exciting.

Join us as we discover potential side hustles and online business ventures that will make the time and energy more rewarding than the average day job. Follow along as we explore the following:

- Learn the significance of active and passive incomes, including how to make the best of both worlds work for you. You will find yourself looking at the working world with open eyes as you realize how few people are making the connection between the two incomes. You will be surprised to discover how easy it is to turn active into passive income and wonder why no one else is doing it.

- Discover whether your passion lies in the marketing industry, such as social media marketing or affiliate marketing. If you are witty, creative, and know how to work for a crowd, your passion may have been marketing all along. Read on to see how fun it is to run social media accounts for companies or for your own business.

- Discover what pitfalls careless marketers have fallen for and learn from their mistakes. You will also learn how to tie certain content into brilliant affiliate marketing. Reap the benefits of promoting other merchants and see how lucrative it is to be a market online.

- Realize your full potential when you dive into the phenomenal experience that is blogging. Share with the world the knowledge and wisdom you have gained in your life. If you are an avid traveler, let fellow enthusiasts know what you have seen, or warn vacation-goers of what to expect in certain locations.

- Turn your passion into a money-making venture. Write about it; take pictures, and share it with the world. Your knowledge and interests are desired and shared by others. Let them know that you exist and broaden your horizons by interacting with people around the world.

You have the potential to turn any interest and passion into a way to make money when you turn to the digital world. There is no need to waste your days bored with work—not when the online world eagerly waits for you to enter and share your contribution. Are you ready to take the next step and make money online?

The Internet is certainly ready to embrace your ideas. Do not hesitate now. Follow along with this book to discover your passions and get started with turning those passions into success.